PROTECTION OF ASSETS

CRISIS MANAGEMENT

PROTECTION
OF ASSETS

CRISIS MANAGEMENT

ASIS International | 1625 Prince Street | Alexandria, VA 22314 USA | *www.asisonline.org*

ACKNOWLEDGMENTS

ASIS International (ASIS), the world's leading society for security professionals, originally founded in 1955 as the American Society for Industrial Security, acquired *Protection of Assets* in December 2003. The acquisition of this work underscores the Society's leadership role in professional education. It is the sincere desire of ASIS and its editorial staff to continue to enhance the value of this important reference.

Protection of Assets, which has been in existence since 1974, is recognized as the premier reference for security professionals and the publisher wishes to acknowledge the two founding authors and subsequent editors.

Timothy J. Walsh, CPP   Richard J. Healy, CPP

———

Timothy L. Williams, CPP
Managing Editor

Editorial Associates

David G. Aggleton, CPP
Milton E. Moritz, CPP
Mike Hodge, J.D.
Sanford Sherizon, Ph.D., CISSP
Timothy J. Walsh, CPP, Editor Emeritus

As we move forward, confronted with issues that present a challenge to the security industry, our mission is to ensure that *Protection of Assets* provides the strategic solutions necessary to help professionals meet the demands of the 21st century and beyond. We also pledge to assemble a group of subject matter experts who will enhance this reference as necessary to achieve our mission.

Michael E. Knoke, CPP
Managing Editor

Eva Giercuszkiewicz, MLS, Project Manager
Evangeline Pappas, Production Manager
Peter E. Ohlhausen, Technical Editor

OBJECTIVES OF *PROTECTION OF ASSETS*

Protection of Assets (POA) is intended for a security professional to find current, accurate, and practical treatment of the broad range of asset protection subjects, strategies, and solutions in a single source.

The need for such a comprehensive resource is quite widespread according to the editors, writers, and many professional colleagues whose advice has been sought in compiling this text. The growing size and frequency of all forms of asset losses, coupled with the related increasing cost and complexity of countermeasures selection, demand a systematic and unified presentation of protection doctrine in all relevant areas, as well as standards and specifications as they are issued. Of course, it would be presumptuous to assume that any small group of authors could present such material unaided. It is, therefore, a fundamental objective of *Protection of Assets* to draw upon as large a qualified source base as can be developed. The writers, peer reviewers, and editors attempt to distill from the available data, common or recurrent characteristics, trends, and other factors, which identify or signal valid protection strategies. The objective is to provide a source document where information on any protection problem can be obtained.

READERSHIP

Protection of Assets is intended for a wide readership: all security professionals and business managers with asset protection responsibility. The coherent discussion and pertinent reference material in each subject area should help the reader conduct unique research that is effective and organized. Of particular significance are the various forms, matrices, and checklists that give the reader a practical start toward application of the security theory to his or her own situation. *POA* also serves as a central reference for students pursuing a program in security or asset protection.

DIALOGUE

We hope that *Protection of Assets* becomes an important source of professional insight for those who read it and that it stimulates serious dialogue between and among security professionals. Any reader who is grappling with an unusual, novel, or difficult security problem and would appreciate the opinions of others is encouraged to write a succinct statement describing the problem and send it to us at ASIS [protectionofassets@asisonline.org]. At the reader's request his identity will not be disclosed, but the problem will be published with invitations for comment. Readers are also encouraged to communicate agreement or disagreement with strategies or applications recommended in *POA* and to suggest alternatives. We reserve the right to publish or refrain from publishing submitted material. The editors also solicit statements of reader opinion on matters of asset protection policy in which a cross-sectional view would be helpful.

SUPPLEMENTAL TRAINING

Readers with supervisory or management responsibility for other security and asset protection personnel will find *POA* to be a useful resource from which to assign required readings. Such readings could be elements of a formal training syllabus and could be assigned as part of related course sessions.

With all these objectives in mind, we present to you *Protection of Assets*, in the sincere belief it will enhance your expertise in the security field.

Michael E. Knoke, CPP
Managing Editor

CONTRIBUTORS

The success of this publication is directly related to the peer review process recognized by most professions. Security professionals, members of academia, and other subject matter experts were involved in contributing current information, conducting research, reviewing submissions, and providing constructive comments so that we are able to provide a publication that is recognized as the "go to" reference for security professionals worldwide.

It is with sincere appreciation that I wish to thank the below-named individuals who contributed to *Protection of Assets*.

Teresa M. Abrahamsohn, CPP	James P. Carino, Jr., CPP	Richard H. Frank, CPP
Sean A. Ahrens, CPP	Sue Carioti	Kenneth M. Freeman, CPP
Marene N. Allison	James S. Cawood, CPP, PCI, PSP	Peter J. French, CPP
Randy I. Atlas, CPP	Richard E. Chase, CPP	Mary Lynn Garcia, CPP
George J. Barletta, CPP	John C. Cholewa, III, CPP	John W. Gehrlein, CPP
Mark H. Beaudry, CPP	Tom M. Conley, CPP	Eva Giercuszkiewicz, MLS
Regis W. Becker, CPP	Geoffrey T. Craighead, CPP	Gregory A. Gilbert, CPP
Brent Belcoff, CPP	Michael A. Crane, J.D., CPP	Frederick G. Giles, CPP
Howard J. Belfor, CPP	Bruce A. Dean, CPP	Timothy D. Giles, CPP, PSP
Adolfo M. Benages, CPP	Fritz X. Delinski	David H. Gilmore, CPP
Lawrence K. Berenson, CPP	Edward P. De Lise, CPP	Christopher Giusti, CPP
Alexander E. Berlonghi	David A. Dobbins, PSP	Brian D. Gouin, PSP
Raymond J. Bernard, PSP	Clifford E. Dow, CPP	Richard P. Grassie, CPP
Henri A. Berube	Christina M. Duffey, CPP	Benjamin P. Greer
Martin T. Biegelman, J.D.	Brandon Dunlap	Steven R. Harris
Daniel E. Bierman, CPP, PSP	Cheryl D. Elliott, CPP, PCI	Ronald D. Heil, CPP
Patrick C. Bishop, CPP	James W. Ellis, CPP, PSP	Richard J. Heffernan, CPP
Dennis R. Blass, CPP, PSP	William R. Etheridge	Chris A. Hertig, CPP
Keith C. Blowe, CPP	Gregory Alan Ewing, CPP, PSP	William T. Hill, CPP
Paul F. Boyarin, CPP, PCI	Kenneth G. Fauth, CPP	Ronald W. Hobbs, CPP
Tom Boyer	Lawrence J. Fennelly	Mark D. Hucker, CPP
Pete Brake, Jr., CPP	Donald J. Fergus	W. Geoffrey Hughes, PCI
Darryl R. Branham, CPP	Eugene F. Ferraro, CPP, PCI	John L. Hunepohl
Joseph P. Buckley, III	James H. Fetzer, III, CPP	Gregory L. Hurd, CPP
Lucien G. Canton, CPP	Michael T. Flachs, CPP	Gregory W. Jarpey, PSP

TABLE OF CONTENTS

PREFACE

CONTRIBUTORS

TABLE OF FIGURES

CHAPTER 1
EMERGENCY MANAGEMENT: THEORY AND PLANNING

1.1 ORIGINS OF EMERGENCY MANAGEMENT

One can imagine cave dwellers practicing a primitive version of emergency management as they reacted to natural disasters and hungry predators. In their world, mitigation may have been nothing more than finding a cave that did not get flooded in a heavy rain. Their idea of preparedness may have been to keep a big rock or a club handy to use against a large animal on the prowl. Response may have been limited to fighting or fleeing, and recovery could have involved the selection of another cave. Without realizing it, the cave dwellers may have been practicing a prehistoric form of what we now refer to as comprehensive emergency management.

History has witnessed many catastrophic events, some resulting from forces of nature and others from human action. They have included droughts, famines, floods, fires, pandemics, volcanic eruptions, earthquakes, tsunamis, and other disasters. While the types of calamities have not changed much, the ways in which people have prepared for, responded to, and recovered from emergencies have evolved over time.

Formal emergency management in the United States can be traced to the beginning of the 19th century when Congress first voted to allocate federal funds in response to a local disaster. From the latter part of that century to the 1930s, federal, state, local, and, in some cases, private-sector action was prompted by fires, earthquakes, and floods. During the Cold War, the federal government established civil defense programs that included public fallout shelters and "duck and cover" drills in schools. By the 1970s, communities were dealing with a variety of federal agencies regarding disaster assistance and relief, with each agency responsible for one aspect of the overall effort. In 1979, the Federal Emergency Management Agency (FEMA) was established through the consolidation of most of the agencies and programs involved in emergency management at the federal level. With the creation of the U.S. Department of Homeland Security (DHS), FEMA initially became the new department's Emergency Preparedness and Response Directorate. As a result of subsequent legislative and DHS action, FEMA's structure, responsibilities, and position within DHS have continued to evolve.

As emergency management evolved, so did the professionalism of those engaged in the field. Part of the increased professionalism was reflected in the development of college and university certificate and degree programs in various aspects of emergency management in the United States and other countries. Some of those programs are available online to students anywhere in the world. In addition, an array of state, provincial, national, and international emergency management organizations has emerged as well. The FEMA Higher Education Program Web site (http://training.fema.gov/EMIWeb/edu/) contains not only a list of emergency management programs in higher education, but also college courses, textbooks, and materials, developed under FEMA's aegis, which are available for download at no charge.

1.2 STUDIES AND RESEARCH

Current practices in emergency management are based, in part, on a variety of standards, guidelines, directives, and reference publications. However, there is no single industry standard and no single glossary of terms accepted by all public- and private-sector organizations. Different references and different organizations may use terms such as *emergency management, emergency planning, crisis and emergency management, disaster preparedness, disaster recovery,* or *business continuity* to refer to some or all of the principles and concepts addressed in this chapter. For ease of reference, the terms *emergency management* and *emergency operations plan* are used to describe the overall principles and concepts addressed herein, except where business continuity and continuity of operations are specifically discussed. In discussions of international emergency management activities, the terminology used by the country or region is maintained. This chapter does not attempt to identify all the references that may be applicable to a given organization or set of conditions.

Much research has been conducted by or under the auspices of FEMA (www.fema.gov), dealing primarily with mitigation programs and strategies related to various natural threats, such as hurricanes, floods, tornadoes, and earthquakes. In the aftermath of the September 11, 2001, terrorist attacks against the United States, research has also been conducted regarding attacks against buildings. Examples include the following:

- Federal Emergency Management Agency, *Reference Manual to Mitigate Terrorist Attacks Against Buildings*, FEMA 426 (2003).

- Federal Emergency Management Agency, *World Trade Center Building Performance Study: Data Collection, Preliminary Observations, and Recommendations*, FEMA 403 (2002).

- National Institute of Standards and Technology, *Key Findings of NIST's June 2004 Progress Report on the Federal Building and Fire Safety Investigation of the World Trade Center Disaster* (2004).

1.3 SCOPE

Some of the concepts and practices developed or adopted by FEMA for use by state and local emergency management authorities can also be applied to emergency management in business. This chapter is addressed to emergency planners and managers in businesses and other organizations. Therefore, it does not address such issues as large-scale community evacuations in the event of hurricanes or the establishment of mass care (food and shelter) for flooding evacuees.

The references cited here are primarily keyed to emergency management practices in the United States, although many of the planning concepts and considerations identified by ASIS International, FEMA, and the National Fire Protection Association (NFPA) may be appropriate in other countries as well. Emergency management and disaster preparedness/response structures, capabilities, and requirements vary from one country to another. Therefore, readers outside the United States should consult their local and national emergency management authorities regarding requirements and practices. While it is not feasible to discuss emergency management arrangements in every country, details in selected countries and regions are addressed below:

- **Canada.** Public Safety and Emergency Preparedness Canada (PS), was established by the Canadian Prime Minister in 2003. The Web site http://www.publicsafety.gc.ca/index-eng.aspx contains information on the Emergency Management Act, which took effect in 2007. PS publishes the *Federal Emergency Response Plan*, January 2011 (http://www.publicsafety.gc.ca/prg/em/ferp-eng.aspx) and *National Emergency Response System*, January 2011, (http://www.publicsafety.gc.ca/prg/em/_fl/ners-eng.pdf), among other documents.

- **United Kingdom.** Responsibility for civil protection and emergency planning rests with the Civil Contingencies Secretariat (CCS), which was established in the Cabinet Office in 2001. The Civil Contingencies Act 2004 updates previous legislation, some dating back to 1920, regarding civil protection and emergency powers. Further information about civil protection and emergency planning in the UK can be obtained from the CCS Web site (http://www.cabinetoffice.gov.uk/content/civil-contingencies) and from UK Resilience (http://www.cabinetoffice.gov.uk/ukresilience). The latter site contains a wealth of information related to UK emergency preparedness, response, and recovery, including a link to the Civil Contingencies Act 2004 and the lead government departments for various types of contingencies. Among other publications, CCS publishes the *Business Continuity Management Toolkit*, available from http://www.direct.gov.uk/en/Governmentcitizensandrights/Dealingwithemergencies/Preparingfor emergencies/DG_175927?IdcService=GET_FILE&dID=189314&Rendition=Web, and *Emergency Preparedness: Guidance on Part 1 of the Civil Contingencies Act 2004*, available at http://www.cabinetoffice.gov.uk/sites/default/files/resources/emergprep final.pdf. A major nongovernmental resource in the UK is British Civil Defence (www.britishcivildefence.org).

- **Australia.** Emergency management at the federal level in Australia is under the purview of the Attorney-General's Department (AGD). AGD publishes the *Australian Emergency Manuals* (AEMs), with titles ranging from *Economic and Financial Aspects of Disaster Recovery* to *Evacuation Planning*. AGD also handles several disaster plans. Information on the AEMs and the disaster plans can be obtained at www.ema.gov.au.

- **New Zealand.** The Ministry of Civil Defence & Emergency Management was created in July 1999. In 2002, the Civil Defence Emergency Management Act took effect. The ministry offers a number of publications, including *Best Practice Guides* and *Director's Guidelines*. More information is available at http://www.civildefence.govt.nz.

- **Caribbean.** The Caribbean Disaster Emergency Response Agency (CDERA) is a regional agency created in 1991. Sixteen Caribbean states are currently represented within CDERA. Its Web site (www.cdera.org) contains information on the agency's activities as well as the regional disaster response levels.

1.4 INTRODUCTION TO EMERGENCY MANAGEMENT

1.4.1 IMPORTANCE OF EMERGENCY MANAGEMENT

Unexpected emergencies and contingencies occur with dismaying regularity. When a disaster or other emergency strikes, many decisions must be made while the event is still unfolding and the true dimensions of the situation are unknown. While some decisions will affect the health of the organization for many years, others may have an immediate effect on its ability to survive at all. An emergency can overwhelm those who have done no planning or preparation. People do not want to believe that bad things could happen to them or their environments. However, just as it is risky not to have health insurance, it is dangerous not to have planned and tested emergency procedures.

Emergency management has taken on greater importance in the 21st century as businesses have been victims of floods, earthquakes, hurricanes, and other natural disasters. Those events, in conjunction with such highly publicized attacks as computer hacking, workplace violence, and the September 11, 2001, terrorist attacks, have demonstrated the need for effective emergency management.

Threats such as the Y2K computer challenge, terrorism, and war have forced businesses to take a more active role in implementing emergency operations plans (EOPs). Effective emergency management programs prepare an enterprise for business interruptions and ensure the proper flow of critical information in a disaster or emergency. Planning is essential to ensure recovery from business interruptions and to protect the profitability of the enterprise.

To a large extent, emergency management is generic. Every emergency requires certain common responses. However, the character of the specific situation must be understood for optimal response. Situation-specific training and equipment are needed for the different kinds of emergencies likely to affect each industry and facility.

Emergency response personnel should be prepared to function in all types of emergencies, even those not anticipated at the time of plan development. Primary training should focus on the most likely situations and the location, construction, size, and function of each site. In large organizations with multiple locations, it is essential to require an overall EOP to ensure proper coordination throughout the various sites. Also needed are specific emergency plans tailored to local sites' particular exposures.

Even with planning, it is necessary to improvise and remain flexible when a disaster or other emergency strikes. The varieties of emergencies make planning for every conceivable contingency impossible; however, general planning and resource allocations are feasible. Adequate planning makes the difference between recovery and the demise of the organization.

For most commercial, industrial, and governmental enterprises, the need to resume normal operations rapidly is as great as the need to control potential damage.

Planning in advance of an emergency is essential. During an emergency, one should expect confusion and an interruption of communication links. Conditions may become chaotic. An emergency plan should enable those responsible for recovery to focus on solving major problems. Because responding promptly to an emergency may prevent it from causing substantial loss, an emergency plan should provide the basis for orderly actions and for making decisions that minimize loss.

The logical beginning of emergency management is the development of a plan that does the following (ASIS, 2003, 2004; MSU, 2002; NFPA, 2010):

- defines "emergency" in terms relevant to the organization

- establishes an organization to perform specific tasks before, during, and after an emergency

- establishes a method for using available resources and for obtaining additional resources at the time of an emergency

- provides a means for moving normal operations into and back out of the emergency mode of operations

1.4.2 ELEMENTS OF EMERGENCY MANAGEMENT

Emergency management is the term for a four-pronged process used by the emergency management community throughout the United States. The four elements of emergency management are mitigation, preparedness, response, and recovery. While this approach to emergency management was originally developed and applied at the state and local government level, the elements can be applied to business continuity as well, with some variations in terminology and implementation. The elements are described as follows (FEMA, 1993, 2007a, 2010a; DHS, n.d.; MSU, 2002; NFPA, 2010):

- **Mitigation.** According to FEMA (2007b), mitigation encompasses

  activities providing a critical foundation in the effort to reduce the loss of life and property from natural and/or manmade disasters by avoiding or lessening the impact of a disaster and providing value to the public by creating safer communities. Mitigation seeks to fix the cycle of disaster damage, reconstruction, and repeated damage. These activities or actions, in most cases, will have a long-term sustained effect.

In the 1996 version of FEMA's all-hazard planning guide, mitigation actions were described as involving

> lasting, often permanent, reduction of exposure to, probability of, or potential loss from hazard events. They tend to focus on where and how to build... Mitigation can also involve educating businesses and the public on simple measures they can take to reduce loss and injury, like fastening bookshelves, water heaters, and file cabinets to walls to keep them from falling during earthquakes.

Although that particular version of the guide is no longer in use, its description of mitigation actions is still a useful way to view the mitigation aspect of emergency management.

- **Preparedness.** This aspect of emergency management encompasses actions taken before an event to plan, organize, equip, train, and exercise in order to deal with emergencies that cannot be avoided or entirely mitigated.

- **Response.** This element entails activities that address the short-term, direct effects of an incident. Response includes immediate actions to save lives, protect property, and meet basic human needs. Response also includes the execution of emergency operations plans and of mitigation activities designed to limit the loss of life, personal injury, property damage, and other unfavorable outcomes. As indicated by the situation, response activities include applying intelligence and other information to lessen the effects or consequences of an incident; increased security operations; continuing investigations into the nature and source of the threat; ongoing public health and agricultural surveillance and testing processes; immunizations, isolation, or quarantine; and specific law enforcement operations aimed at preempting, interdicting, or disrupting illegal activity and apprehending actual perpetrators and bringing them to justice (FEMA, 2007b).

- **Recovery.** This aspect involves near-term and long-term actions taken to return the organization to a pre-emergency level of operation or, in some cases, to a new level of operation. Recovery efforts may include implementation of continuity of operation or business resumption plans, activation of emergency relocation sites, and reconstitution or restoration at the original location or a new permanent location.

Business continuity (BC) is, in many respects, the private-sector version of emergency management, with some additional actions, such as a business impact analysis (BIA), that are not applicable to communities. BC encompasses all the actions taken by a business before, during, or after an emergency to minimize the emergency's negative impact on the organization's operations and to bring about a timely response, resumption of critical business functions, and recovery if an emergency does occur. Although the definitions and methodology may vary somewhat from one BC reference to another, the underlying concepts are generally similar. While business continuity is keyed to the private sector, it can be used by governmental entities to reduce the impact on their own critical functions (ASIS, 2005).

Continuity of operations or COOP is a term normally applied specifically to the U.S. federal government. COOP is different from BC in that COOP entails movement of critical functions and personnel to an alternate operating site or sites in accordance with a pre-established COOP plan.

1.4.3 OBJECTIVES OF EMERGENCY MANAGEMENT

Emergency management has three primary objectives. The first is to minimize the probability of a threat or emergency. This may be possible with human or accidental threats; however, it is not achievable with natural threats, such as hurricanes, tornadoes, and snowstorms. Therefore, the second objective is to mitigate the impact if the event occurs. The final, equally important objective is to recover from the emergency and resume normal operations. Normalcy after an emergency will be quite different among victims. Therefore, the two key elements necessary to achieve the objectives are what is to be done and who is to do it. An effective tool for determining the probability of a threat or a disaster, and its impact on an organization, is to conduct a risk analysis in the development stage of the emergency plan.

1.5 PLANNING ISSUES AND CONSIDERATIONS

1.5.1 TYPES OF THREATS AND CONTINGENCIES

The emergencies or contingencies for which plans may be developed can be grouped into three major categories: natural, human (either internal or external), and accidental. Natural threats include all weather-related emergencies, such as hurricanes, tornadoes, floods, winter storms, and fires caused by lightning, as well as non-weather natural events, such as earthquakes and volcanic eruptions. Human threats are deliberate adverse actions and events, such as terrorist activity, arson, civil disorder, and barricade or hostage situations. Accidental threats are non-deliberate adverse actions and events, such as hazardous material spills and telecommunications and computer outages. The various types of threats represent a range of contingencies for which planning is appropriate.

Emergency plans are not intended to cover situations addressed in the normal course of business or government operations. For example, if a key individual is sick, on vacation, or traveling, someone else can take over that person's responsibilities in accordance with the organization's normal operating procedures. However, if the bulk of the work force is unable to reach the work site due to a major weather emergency, or if a hurricane or tornado seriously damages the facility, a non-routine situation exists, for which planning is essential (ASIS, 2005).

Emergencies for which planning is appropriate include the following, among others (FEMA, 1993; NFPA, 2010; OSHA, 2001):

- fire
- explosion
- water outage
- power outage
- computer system failure
- telecommunications failure
- fuel leak
- hazmat (hazardous materials) incident
- bomb incident
- civil disorder

- armed attack
- barricade/hostage incident
- severe weather
  — tornado
  — hurricane
  — thunderstorm
  — flood
- other natural occurrences
  — earthquake
  — volcano

1.5.2 **TYPES OF EMERGENCY PLANS**

The threats or emergencies listed above can be translated into the types of emergency plans shown below. Not every organization needs all these plans; it depends on the nature of the organization's activities, the organization's criticality, its attractiveness as a target, its location, and the types of facilities it occupies, among other considerations. Furthermore, the all-hazards approach to planning, explained below, should be employed to the maximum extent. The following are some types of emergency plans (Broder, 2006; FEMA, 2010a; NFPA, 2010):

- bomb incident plan
- fire plan
- medical emergency plan
- workplace violence/trauma plan
- hazmat response plan
- utility outage plan
- computer system failure plan
- telecommunications failure plan
- severe weather plan
- continuity of operations (COOP) plan
- business resumption/recovery plan

1.5.3 **PLANNING FORMATS AND ALL-HAZARDS PLANNING**

Emergency Operations Plan

The specific emergency planning format used in a given organization depends on the nature of the organization and the organization's policy. The all-hazards approach has been adopted by FEMA and can be used in business and organizational plans as well as community plans. The approach provides for a basic emergency plan, or emergency operations plan (EOP), with functional annexes (such as emergency call lists) that apply to multiple emergency situations, and threat-specific annexes (such as procedures for bomb incidents). This approach recognizes that many planning requirements are similar regardless of whether an incident is a natural threat, a human threat, or an accident. For example, an evacuation plan is necessary for fires, bomb incidents, and hazmat spills.

FEMA has developed a number of hazard-specific planning considerations dealing with fire, hazmat incidents, floods and flash floods, hurricanes, tornadoes, severe winter storms, earthquakes, and technological emergencies (Broder, 2006; FEMA, 1993, 2010a). Bomb incidents, including bomb threats, actual or suspected improvised explosive devices (IEDs), and detonations or deflagrations should be addressed in an annex to the emergency plan. Specific information regarding these incidents can be found in Chapter 3.

An alternative planning approach involves developing stand-alone plans for each relevant emergency or contingency. A third approach can be some combination of the first two. Regardless of the format, the plan should be developed in the simplest way possible, with outlines of the specific responsibilities for those assigned to emergency response. This ensures an effective response to any extraordinary situation.

Two significant considerations arise in choosing a planning format. The first pertains to the dissemination of the plan. A plan is of little value if it is not readily available to those whom it affects. Therefore, the format should facilitate the distribution of the plan to all individuals and organizational elements with designated responsibilities under the plan. The second consideration involves the maintenance of the plan. To be effective, every emergency plan should be reviewed and updated regularly.

A formal audit of the plan should be conducted at least annually. In addition, the plan should be evaluated and modified as required after the following:

- each training drill
- each emergency
- changes in personnel or their responsibilities
- changes in the facility's physical design
- changes in policies or procedures

Emergency planning software and some off-the-shelf database programs can facilitate incorporating the changes into and disseminating the amended plan (ASIS, 2005; FEMA, 1993; NFPA, 2010). It is essential that all emergency plans are reviewed at least once a year, to ensure that all dynamic information, such as floor plans, contact numbers, key personnel, and key assets, are accurate.

The planning format directly affects the updating process. For example, if an organization uses the all-hazards approach, it is relatively simple to update and disseminate information common to multiple emergencies, such as emergency contact numbers. On the other hand, if an organization has chosen to publish a series of stand-alone plans, it will have to update every plan each time common points of contact or emergency numbers change (Broder, 2006; FEMA, 2010a).

Other Emergency Plans

An EOP developed with the all-hazards approach will address the preparedness and response aspects of business continuity. Mitigation strategies related to constructing or retrofitting facilities or otherwise reducing the impact of potential emergency events should be addressed in a separate mitigation plan.

Similarly, business resumption/recovery plans and continuity of operations plans should be separate from the organization's security operations plan (FEMA, 2010a; NFPA, 2010).

1.5.4 DEVELOPMENT OF THE PLAN

Developing and implementing a plan to cope with possible emergencies is a time-consuming process. Software tools, especially those based on a relational database system, can significantly reduce the labor of capturing the necessary information. Emergency management consultants can also help ensure a complete plan. However, neither software nor consultants can reduce the need for responsible participation by the organization's management team in plan preparation. Management has to be directly involved in the identification and evaluation of the organizational assets as part of the plan development. This process will identify the key assets of the organization that need to be protected. Managers directly involved in day-to-day operations can make risk analysis more manageable.

The purpose of an emergency plan is to highlight the types of problems that decision makers and other key emergency management personnel will encounter and to require them to consider, in advance, how to react when an emergency develops (ASIS, 2005, 2009; NFPA, 2010).

1.5.5 **PLANNING PROCESS**

The planning process is critical and often misunderstood. Far too often, if plans are developed at all, they are put on the shelf and forgotten. For a plan to be effective, it must reflect the requirements of the organization to which it pertains. Furthermore, all persons tasked with responsibilities must clearly understand their responsibilities and be trained to fulfill them.

In addition, the plan must be tested through practice, and it should be revised in light of such testing. An exercise or an actual implementation of the plan may point to the need for revisions, reassignment of responsibilities, or retraining of personnel, after which the plan should be retested. The most important thing about planning: it is a continuing process that is never finished as long as the plan exists (ASIS, 2005, 2009; FEMA, 1993; NFPA, 2010).

1.5.6 **TRAINING, DRILLS, AND EXERCISES**

All businesses need to plan initial and refresher emergency training. The scope of the training depends on the nature of the entity's activities. However, OSHA (2001) has identified certain topics that should be covered with all employees. In addition to employees, businesses should consider the training and orientation needs of recurring visitors, contractors, and others who have frequent access to the facilities. In areas involving hazardous activities, additional requirements apply.

Training and orientation must be reinforced and tested with periodic drills and exercises. These may include the following:

- tabletop exercises conducted in a conference room for members of the organization's crisis management team (CMT) or other management personnel

- evacuation and shelter-in-place drills for all employees

- walk-through of an emergency plan or particular emergency response functions by selected organizational personnel

- a full exercise involving outside response agencies

Emergency tests and exercises are conducted for many reasons:

- checking the workability of a plan or a part thereof

- determining the level of staff awareness and training

- evaluating the adequacy of emergency communications

- identifying shortcomings in evacuation procedures

Not every part of a plan needs to be checked simultaneously. However, each exercise should be designed to evaluate one or more aspects of the emergency plan and its implementation. To validate an organization's emergency plan, an unannounced test should be conducted with appropriate controls and safeguards in place.

Security tests and exercises are rehearsals for the real event and, subject to safety concerns, should be keyed to the actual security plan to the maximum extent possible. A rehearsal for a play uses the same script as an actual performance; a security exercise should be no different. One of the least desirable outcomes of emergency planning exercises is to cause employees to think "This is only a test" or "We simulate doing X, Y, and Z when we do a drill." The rule should always be: *Train to the plan and exercise the plan.*

Figure 1-1 offers recommendations for developing and conducting exercises of emergency plans. Exercises should be realistic but should not put people at risk. In particular, the use of force by armed security personnel and by any role players must be carefully controlled.

- Consider a logical sequence of exercise complexity (paper, sand table, interactive, full-up), depending on the needs of the organization.

- Train the trainers first, and make sure they understand that exercises are not competitions.

- To make it easier to deal with a range of emergencies, design the training and exercise program so that it takes into account, but is not limited to, the worst-case scenarios.

- Realize that safety and use of force are primary controlling factors.

- Understand that an exercise can deal with one part of a plan rather than the entire plan.

- Train to the plan and then exercise the plan.

- Develop the scenario based on the plan, or part thereof, to be tested.

- Control communications to external agencies.

- Have a plan to deal with real-world incidents during the exercise.

- Keep exercises as realistic as possible within safety limits.

- Exercise alternate decision makers, alternate exits, and alternate routes.

Prepared by David H. Gilmore, CPP. Used with permission.

Figure 1-1
Exercise Planning Recommendations

Another important consideration involves notifying external agencies. Emergency response agencies outside the organization should not be contacted during an exercise unless they are involved in the exercise. It is important to avoid inadvertent emergency responses that could put emergency responders and bystanders at risk. An alternative is to have exercise players log the external contacts they would make or, alternatively, describe them to an exercise controller or umpire (ASIS, 2003, 2004, 2005, 2009; Broder, 2006; FEMA, 1993; MSU, 2002; NFPA, 2010; NOD, 2009a; OSHA, 2001).

1.5.7 SPECIAL PLANNING NEEDS

Emergency plans should account for personnel with disabilities, including those of vision, hearing, mental function, and mobility. The National Organization on Disability (NOD) emphasizes the need to engage those with disabilities in planning and testing. The U.S. Department of Labor's Office of Disability Employment Policy (ODEP) has published a report offering ideas applicable to non-federal entities, even though it is geared to federal managers (FEMA, 2010b; NOD, 2009a, 2009b; OSHA, 2001).

1.5.8 COMPONENTS OF AN EMERGENCY OPERATIONS PLAN

The components of an emergency operations plan vary depending on the planning format in use, the emergency/contingency for which the plan is being developed, and the needs of the organization to which the plan pertains. A plan may include all the elements shown in Figure 1-2, and it may also include additional specialized or organization-specific components. In the final analysis, the plan must fit the emergencies that may be encountered.

• Purpose	• Family/victim support
• Priorities	• Medical services
• Planning assumptions	• Emergency evacuation and shelter-in-place
• Impact	• Emergency shutdown and restoration
• Operational tasks and procedures	• Resources and logistics
• Pre-event	• Notifications and communications
• During event	• Records and reports
• Post-event	• Training and testing
• Command/management and control	• Appendices
• External liaison and coordination	
• Public affairs/media relations	

Prepared by David H. Gilmore, CPP. Used with permission.

Figure 1-2
Components of Emergency Operations Plan

1.5.9 **PRIORITIES**

In constructing an EOP, planners should consider the relative importance of different types of activities. Without an advance determination of priorities, resources will be wasted. Each organization must set its own priorities. The following is one possible list:

1. Protect human life.

2. Prevent or minimize personal injury.

3. Reduce the exposure of assets.

4. Optimize loss control for assets whose exposure cannot be reduced.

5. Restore normal operations as quickly as possible.

In setting priorities, certain time-tested principles should be applied to the protection of life. Those principles include the following:

- **Evacuation and shelter.** Move all persons not needed in disaster operations to places of safety.

- **Personal protection.** Ensure that persons who must remain in a threatened area are as well-protected as possible.

- **Rescue and relief.** Provide a ready means of support and assistance for injured persons.

For preventing or minimizing injury, the following are some guiding principles:

- **Design safety.** Eliminate in advance conditions that increase the likelihood of injury given the nature of the emergency and the character of the organization or facility.

- **Training.** Prepare those who will deal with the disaster so they will not increase their exposure through ignorance or ineptitude.

To reduce exposure of physical assets, a business should conduct good housekeeping and keep valuable materials or equipment from being needlessly concentrated in high-hazard locales. (For example, redundant or backup computers should not be located in the same fire zone as primary computers.) Given sufficient warning time, valuable items can be relocated if provisions have been made for a relocation site and means of transportation.

To control losses, a business needs emergency response systems (people, equipment, and procedures) that can rapidly deploy to threatened locations and be supported operationally. To restore normal operations quickly, it may be necessary to relocate some groups or functions and to revise previous schedules and programs. The data needed to make such determinations must be current and easily accessible (ASIS, 2005, 2009; FEMA, 1993; OSHA, 2001).

Planning assumptions reduce the number of "what ifs"; however, it may be dangerous to assume away certain problems or issues. An example of such an assumption would be that enough vehicles will be available to support an emergency relocation of headquarters. This assumption tells everyone there is no need to make any special provisions for relocation transport. Planning assumptions should not be developed arbitrarily.

Another type of assumption sets forth the parameters under which the plan was developed and identifies issues that must be taken into account by planners. An example of this type of assumption would be that at any given time on a business day, at least 40 percent of the assigned vehicles will be in use off-site or will be unavailable for dispatch due to maintenance.

This assumption puts everyone on notice that, for planning purposes, there is a finite number of vehicles (no more than 60 percent of the total assigned). Another example would be that upon notification about a suspicious device, the bomb squad may take up to 45 minutes to reach the facility. This assumption indicates a condition over which the organization has no control—namely, the speed at which the bomb squad can respond. However, the assumption alerts everyone involved to expect at least a 45-minute interval before the bomb squad reaches the facility and begins to deal with the device (Broder, 2006; FEMA, 2010a).

1.6 COMMAND/MANAGEMENT AND CONTROL

1.6.1 EMERGENCY MANAGEMENT STRUCTURE

One operating official should be designated as the organization's emergency coordinator to assume responsibility for the plan and to ensure that physical department boundaries do not impede a smooth emergency response. The coordinator should be someone regularly responsible for handling emergencies, such as the head of security or engineering. The coordinator should be capable of dealing effectively with management and employees at all levels in the organization. To be most effective, this appointment should be documented in an organizational policy statement that outlines the coordinator's responsibilities and authority. As with any other critical assignment, the top management of the enterprise must give complete support to the program and to the individual selected to organize it. There should also be a designated alternate, by name or position, so there will be no gap in plan maintenance.

The individual responsible for program development should provide coordination and general direction within the organization. Therefore, he or she should prepare appropriate policy and administrative directives to be issued by management to properly establish the program.

A committee of representatives from critical departments or divisions should be appointed to help the coordinator organize the plan. Departments usually represented on such a committee are those critical to the organization and should, at a minimum, include legal, personnel, medical, transportation, public relations, facility engineering, information technology, and security. A totally new organization should not be developed to handle emergencies. Such problems should be handled by the existing organization, temporarily reconfigured, along with executives responsible for the day-to-day operation of the enterprise (ASIS, 2005, 2009; Broder, 2006; FEMA, 1993; NFPA, 2010).

Alternate Designations

One of the most important considerations in developing an emergency management structure is to designate alternates for the primary decision maker and for anyone else who is charged, by name or position, with a particular responsibility under the plan. If possible, more than one alternate should be designated for each primary individual. It is equally important to brief, train, and test the primary and alternate individuals on their assigned duties. These constitute some of the most significant aspects of the planning process, but they are also some of the most challenging for the emergency planner to fulfill because proper training and testing are time-and resource-intensive and are often not given a high priority by management. Nonetheless, training and testing should be conducted before an incident (Broder, 2006; FEMA, 1993; NFPA, 2010).

1.6.2 INCIDENT COMMAND/MANAGEMENT

The Incident Command System (ICS) is a command and control mechanism used by many public safety agencies and jurisdictions in the United States. ICS provides an expandable structure that can be used as needed to manage emergency agencies. Although some of the details vary by jurisdiction, ICS normally consists of five primary elements:

- command
- operations
- planning
- logistics
- finance and administration

Several special staff positions, including public affairs, safety, and liaison, report directly to the incident commander (IC) when the emergency warrants establishment of those positions.

If an incident requires a public safety response, the incident commander is normally the senior member of the responding agency. In many cases, the response may involve only one agency and one jurisdiction. In such a case, ICS, if it needs to be formally implemented due to the size of the incident, would be single-incident command. However, if the incident involves multiple agencies or multiple jurisdictions, then unified command (UC) is typically established. Under UC, there is a collaborative approach to decision-making and a single incident command post, with the agencies involved in the incident participating in the process through direct representation or through the ICS liaison officer, as appropriate. The participating agencies may choose to operate with a single IC, who would normally be the senior representative of the lead agency or jurisdiction.

While ICS has typically been used by public sector agencies, it can serve the private sector as well. According to MSU (2002, p. 17), ICS

> should be understood and practiced by the private sector[,] and the public sector should be aware of the private sector emergency response procedures, which may vary within the business community.

Furthermore, all organizations should have an internal incident management system because not all emergencies require a public safety response. For example, a weather emergency may entail implementation of an organization's emergency operations plan and the activation of its incident management system but will probably not involve any public safety response. The nature and scope of the emergency ultimately determines the organization's level of response. Some limited emergencies may be handled by the organization's emergency coordinator or facility manager without the need for a more robust operation. More extensive emergencies may dictate use of the organization's or facility's incident management system, supported by the organization's crisis management team (CMT). Because the organization's CMT fulfills a strategic rather than tactical role, an emergency that calls for an on-scene incident manager or commander will warrant activation of the organization's incident management system. In that case, the organization's incident commander or manager and supporting personnel will manage the organization's response at the scene, and the CMT will provide necessary support.

In addition, in incidents necessitating a public safety response, the organization's CMT and incident management structure should be prepared to cooperate with the responding agencies and the public safety incident commander, particularly by providing information about the facility and its personnel.

In March 2004, the U.S. Department of Homeland Security (DHS) announced the establishment of the National Incident Management System (NIMS). As DHS observed in the latest version of NIMS (2008):

> The National Incident Management System provides a systematic, proactive approach guiding departments and agencies at all levels of government, the private sector, and nongovernmental organizations to work seamlessly to prepare for, prevent, respond to, recover from, and mitigate the effects of incidents, regardless of cause, size, location, or complexity, in order to reduce the loss of life, property, and harm to the environment.

DHS has also established a National Response Framework (DHS, n.d.), which is

> a guide that details how the Nation conducts all-hazards response—from the smallest incident to the largest catastrophe. This document establishes a comprehensive, national, all-hazards approach to domestic incident response. The Framework identifies the key response principles, as well as the roles and structures that organize national response. It describes how communities, States, the Federal Government and private-sector and nongovernmental partners apply these principles for a coordinated, effective national response. In addition, it describes special circumstances where the Federal Government exercises a larger role, including incidents where Federal interests are involved and catastrophic incidents where a State would require significant support. It lays the groundwork for first responders, decision-makers and supporting entities to provide a unified national response.

The National Response Framework is available at http://www.fema.gov/pdf/emergency/nrf/nrf-core.pdf.

1.6.3 CRISIS OR EMERGENCY MANAGEMENT TEAM

As previously indicated, an organization should avoid establishing a totally new organization to handle most emergencies. The organization's CMT or similar team may include representatives from all of the following components of the organization, depending on the nature of the emergency:

- senior management
- plans and operations
- public affairs
- human resources
- facilities engineering
- security
- safety and occupational health
- legal counsel

- resource management

- logistics

- chaplain (if available)

- employee union

Just as the composition of the CMT varies depending on the type of incident, so do the responsibilities of the CMT. Those duties may include the following, among others:

- coordinating implementation of appropriate contingency plans

- coordinating resources and support needed by responding agencies

- coordinating with internal and external agencies, as required

- developing alternative courses of action for presentation to decision makers

- developing a media management strategy and preparing appropriate press releases regarding the incident

- maintaining contact with victims and family members, as appropriate

While some of those duties are common to a number of emergencies, others apply only to certain types of emergencies. In the case of a normal winter weather emergency, the first three duties, and perhaps the fourth, need to be addressed, but the remainder do not apply (ASIS, 2005, 2009; FEMA, 1993; MSU, 2002; NFPA, 2010).

1.6.4 **EMERGENCY OPERATIONS CENTERS AND COMMAND POSTS**

A business should identify a location for use as an emergency operations center (EOC) or crisis management center (CMC) from which the emergency response can be directed. The size, nature, and location of the organization may dictate the location and scope of its EOC/CMC. Small organizations may manage emergencies from the building manager's office, plant manager's office, or other individual's normal work area, while larger organizations may use a conference room or even a dedicated EOC/CMC that is used only in emergencies. During an emergency, the personnel managing the response to the event need to maintain full concentration on coordinating the response; therefore, access to the EOC/CMC should be controlled.

Regardless of the arrangement, the organization should also designate one or more alternate locations, including one in a building other than the one that contains the primary EOC/CMC, in case the primary location is damaged, is destroyed, or becomes inaccessible.

The primary and alternate EOC/CMC locations should be able to accommodate the CMT and should provide redundant communications capabilities. In addition, the locations should have backup power and an independent supply of potable water. Sanitary arrangements that are not dependent on the normal water system must also be considered. In an extended emergency or one in which it is not feasible for CMT members to leave the facility, arrangements will be needed for lodging and feeding CMT members and support personnel (ASIS, 2003, 2004, 2005, 2009; Broder, 2006; FEMA, 1993; MSU, 2000; NFPA, 2010).

1.6.5 COMMUNICATIONS

According to the ASIS International *Emergency Planning Handbook* (2003, p. 46), "One of the most important ingredients in effectively managing an emergency event is communications."

Interoperability, or the ability of different agencies and different jurisdictions to communicate with one another via wireless means, is a significant issue in the public safety community. DHS has launched a major public safety interoperability initiative called SAFECOM. Information about the program can be obtained at the DHS communications (http://www.dhs.gov/files/programs/communications.shtm).

The telephone numbers of law enforcement and fire departments, as well as those of all other emergency services, should be readily available at all times to avoid delay in calling them. In an emergency, the telephones of emergency services may be jammed with calls from other organizations and individuals. For this reason, private-line numbers should be obtained so they may be used in emergencies. If possible, telephones should be programmed to store these numbers and dial them with a limited number of digital inputs. Because an emergency results in many persons simultaneously trying to place telephone calls into or out of the affected location, it is useful to have one or more FX or foreign exchange lines available to the emergency response team. These lines are separate from the local central telephone office that normally serves the facility (ASIS, 2003, 2004, 2005, 2009; Broder, 2006; FEMA, 1993; NFPA, 2010).

1.6.6 COMMAND/MANAGEMENT SUCCESSION

An emergency can occur at any time under any operating conditions. The plan must ensure that a senior management representative is always available to take charge. In emergencies that develop during non-working hours, telephone communications and electrical power may be severed, preventing contact with the appropriate executives and making road travel to the facility impossible. Therefore, initial implementation of the plan and control of the facility may rest with the senior manager present at the site, who in some cases may be a security manager, security supervisor, or security officer. The plan should clearly define responsibilities and indicate how the individual on-site can take charge until a senior manager arrives to assume responsibility.

A list of emergency telephone numbers for key personnel is also essential. This list should be included in the published emergency plan and updated regularly. Distribution of the published plan with the telephone list should be limited to control centers and senior personnel with plan implementation responsibilities. This will ensure as much privacy as possible for individuals who have unlisted numbers or desire a limited release.

In some organizations, emergency succession lists, as opposed to emergency contact lists, are sealed and stored in a safe place, opened only in a major emergency. In others, the succession lists are recorded in the written emergency plans, and those involved with the plan know who is in charge at all times. Some board resolutions provide that the chief executive officer is responsible for the preparation and revision of succession lists to ensure that a management representative is always available to make decisions during an emergency. Emergency succession provisions do not necessarily need to reflect the anticipated normal management succession. The boards of directors in some corporations have established a management succession list for the corporate level as well as for subsidiaries. The board decisions may take the form of resolutions. If alternates are named to the board who have not been formally elected by the shareholders, the plan should be reviewed by counsel to ensure that actions taken in an emergency are lawful.

Some organizations ensure that the board can function even if a large-scale disaster incapacitates so many board members that a quorum is no longer possible. The bylaws of such companies provide a means of returning the board to full strength. One method is for board vacancies to be filled by the remaining board members. Some states have passed special statutes to facilitate emergency planning by corporate organizations. Such provisions should be used if available.

Within government organizations, it is important to ensure that at all times, members of the organization are aware of their individual chain of command/supervision and the name or position of the individual who will succeed their supervisor or manager. In nongovernmental organizations, it is essential that management succession be determined and be available to key personnel in an emergency (ASIS, 2003, 2004, 2005, 2009; FEMA, 1993; NFPA, 2010).

1.7 LIAISON AND COORDINATION

1.7.1 PLANNING LIAISON

Planners should take a wide range of agencies and individuals into account when developing an emergency plan. Examples include the following:

- emergency response personnel (law enforcement, fire, emergency medical services, explosive ordnance disposal, and emergency management agencies)
- senior management and department heads in the organizations to which the plan applies
- other employees
- victims, survivors, and their family members
- elected officials
- other government officials
- media
- neighboring private- and public-sector organizations and community groups
- protesters or activists

Information that may be obtained from some of these entities and from other organizations can be of great value in developing and implementing the emergency plan. In addition, contacts within those groups can help emergency planners obtain assistance and coordinate plans (FEMA, 1993; MSU, 2000).

1.7.2 EMERGENCY RESPONSE AGENCIES

For each emergency response agency that may respond to incidents at the affected facility, emergency planners should answer the following questions:

- Where is it?
- What support can it provide?
- Under what conditions will it respond?
- How fast can it respond?
- What does it need from the planning organization?
- How can it be contacted?
- Is there a written agreement between the organization and the emergency response agency?
- Have representatives from the agency visited the facility?

The last question raises one of the most important considerations in coordinating emergency support. As the 1999 Columbine High School shooting incident in Jefferson County, Colorado, shows, it is imperative that emergency response agencies be aware of the layout and peculiarities of the major facilities to which they may have to respond (FEMA, 1993; MSU, 2000).

1.7.3 MUTUAL AID

In a mutual aid association, businesses and other organizations agree to assist each other by providing materials, equipment, and personnel for disaster control during emergencies. The purpose of such an association is to establish a workable emergency management organization that minimizes damage and ensures the continued operation or early restoration of damaged facilities. The association benefits the community as a whole because its emergency plan is part of the community's total emergency plan. In forming a mutual aid association, organizations' emergency planners usually take the following steps:

1. Obtain the advice, assistance, and guidance of the local government representative responsible for disaster planning.

2. Invite local industries, utilities, and other businesses to send representatives to an organizational meeting.

3. Arrange to have the group addressed by someone experienced in the operation of a mutual aid association.

4. Elect association officers and appoint a coordinator.

5. Appoint committees to develop plans and procedures for various aspects of mutual aid operations, such as membership and bylaws, traffic and security control, fire protection, communications, etc.

6. Schedule periodic meetings.

Government agencies often use interagency support agreements or memoranda of understanding to delineate the support provided among agencies in particular contingencies (ASIS, 2003, 2004, 2005, 2009; MSU, 2000; NFPA, 2010).

1.7.4 PUBLIC AFFAIRS/MEDIA RELATIONS

Disasters and other emergencies are fodder for news representatives, who ask for information immediately. To avoid confusion, the emergency plan should provide for the orderly release of information, preferably through a single source in the organization. The existing public or community relations division may perform this function. Procedures should ensure that the public relations director and alternates are regularly updated on developments by the organization's emergency coordinator.

As soon as news representatives make contact, they should be told what has occurred through prepared press releases and oral briefings. It is best to avoid answering questions with the phrase "no comment." If the media gain the impression that the organization is not releasing adequate information, they may contact individuals far removed from the actual situation who have little or no information. That approach leads to the propagation of rumors, conjecture, and speculation. A public impression that the organization is hiding something could produce a lasting, unfavorable view of the organization.

Press representatives usually cooperate if they understand why the enterprise must limit the release of information. For example, safety considerations might make it necessary to limit access to the disaster area. If so, the problem should be explained, and individuals who have been in the area should be available for interviews. The names of those who have been killed or injured should be released as soon as possible. Press representatives understand that relatives must be informed before such information can be released to the public. The handling of information concerning casualties is an important aspect of internal human relations as well as public relations. The method of handling this information should be defined and included in the written emergency plan.

Organizations should be prepared for media requests for interviews with subject matter experts on specialized issues. In an ongoing incident, such as a barricade or hostage situation, one should expect the perpetrators to be monitoring the local and national media. Organizations should also be prepared to deal with media logistics in the event of an extended incident. It may be necessary to provide a location for media briefings and filings, offer tours of the incident scene, issue media credentials, establish media access control points, or provide a parking area for microwave remote vehicles.

Photographic coverage of the incident scene is important for insurance purposes and to support legal claims. Photographs and videos can be taken by the organization's photographers, or arrangements can be made to obtain copies of photographs taken by news photographers (ASIS, 2003, 2004, 2005, 2009; FEMA, 1993; MSU, 2000, NFPA, 2010).

1.7.5 FAMILY AND VICTIM SUPPORT

Aiding the welfare and morale of employees and their families can pose a serious challenge in an emergency. The American Red Cross and FEMA can provide assistance and guidance in that regard.

Not all emergencies require provisions for family or victim support, but when such help is called for (for example, after a building collapse with trapped victims), the organization should be prepared to deal with fearful, distraught, or angry victims and family members. There should be a designated organizational point of contact for family members and victims. This individual should ensure that family members and victims are informed of the efforts taken to resolve the incident. The organization should also plan for family and victim logistics, addressing such issues as the following:

- establishing a family and victim support center away from any media facilities

- providing food, beverages, and temporary lodging

- providing counseling or pastoral support

- providing transportation to the incident site, if appropriate

As major aviation accidents have graphically illustrated, the manner in which family members and victims are treated attracts media scrutiny. Any missteps in this matter may have an extremely negative effect on public perception of the organization (ASIS, 2005, 2009).

1.7.6 EMERGENCY MEDICAL SERVICES

Immediate and short-term care of the injured may have to be provided by the medical personnel, if any, who are already present in the organization. While some industrial facilities and many military installations have in-house medical support, most public- and private-sector facilities do not (other than perhaps an occupational health nurse). Even where on-site support exists, the medical personnel may not be available every day or at all times of the day. Furthermore, they may not have an emergency transport capability. Therefore, in developing the medical services portion of an emergency plan, planners should first ascertain the type and capabilities of any in-house medical support. They should ask in-house medical personnel to define their capabilities and the conditions under which they can be called upon to provide emergency support. For organizations with in-house medical support, adequate medical supplies must be provided to treat the injured properly. The plan should include provisions to obtain additional supplies from local medical supply houses or other facilities in the area.

Some organizations have selected personnel who are trained to administer basic first aid, including cardiopulmonary resuscitation (CPR), pending the arrival of emergency medical personnel. Other organizations rely solely on local emergency medical services (EMS) personnel. If an organization chooses to have some employees trained in first aid, it is necessary to determine the scope of training administered, the employees to train, and the medical equipment to keep on hand. In doing so, the organization should consult legal counsel regarding liability, licensing, and certification issues. Excellent training can be obtained from the American Red Cross and its local affiliates.

Emergency planners should contact local hospitals to determine the number of emergency patients each can accommodate and the types of treatment available. Not every hospital has complete treatment facilities for every type of illness or injury. For example, burn victims require special treatment, and only a limited number of hospitals have facilities to treat such cases.

Planners must also consider how to transport victims to hospitals or treatment centers. The number of ambulances available in the area should be determined, and arrangements should be made with ambulance company representatives. Because the available ambulances might not be able to handle all the victims or might not be able to reach the facility, emergency planners should develop backup plans to use the organization's own vehicles to transport the injured.

For a mass casualty situation, space must be designated for triage, where trained medical personnel evaluate the injured and prioritize them for treatment. Temporary hospital facilities within the enterprise may have to be provided for victims whom local hospitals cannot accommodate or for those who cannot be moved because of the nature of their injuries. Sufficient space for such emergency medical facilities should be designated in the emergency plan. Under favorable climatic conditions, temporary medical facilities can be erected in tents outdoors.

In planning for an outside emergency medical response to a facility with multiple points of entry, planners should consider the most appropriate points of ingress and egress and most direct routes within the facility. For example, if a school, hotel, or industrial plant has multiple wings and multiple entry points, it will save time if the responding personnel can be directed to the closest entry point. Within the facility, the movement of gurneys needs to be considered, particularly in multi-story buildings. Therefore, planners should consider the location of public, staff, and freight elevators in developing medical emergency plans.

In addition to immediate and short-term medical care, planners should consider the availability of post-incident medical care. In addition, depending on the nature of the incident, it may be necessary to make provisions for trauma counseling and other psychological assistance, both during and after the incident, not only for victims and their family members but also for emergency responders (ASIS, 2003, 2004; FEMA, 1993, 2010a; OSHA, 2001, 2004).

1.7.7 **SECURITY AND FIRE PROTECTION**

It should not be assumed that local law enforcement and fire services will assist with every emergency. They might be unable to respond because of impassable roads or insufficient personnel to assist all organizations in need. Depending on the nature and location of the organization, the emergency plan may need to provide for additional employees who can assist those regularly assigned to security and fire protection duties. Total self-sufficiency may be required, at least for a limited period. However, with regard to fire and rescue operations, a distinction needs to be made between industrial and non-industrial facilities. Industrial facilities may have a volunteer in-house fire and rescue operation; however, non-industrial facilities, particularly office buildings, operate differently. Their occupants are typically instructed to identify the problem, notify the appropriate authorities, and evacuate the affected area.

It is desirable for local fire department personnel to inspect a facility to identify hazardous conditions that could increase losses during an emergency and to recommend corrective actions. They should also visit the facility to become familiar with the layout and the location of any hazardous materials. The site's emergency planners should provide them with telephone numbers for key management personnel and periodically updated floor plans for training purposes. A survey of neighboring installations should be conducted regularly to ascertain the existence of any potential hazards (such as chemicals) or other conditions that could exacerbate the impact of a crisis.

The local law enforcement agency should be invited to participate in a tour of the facility and should be given a drawing that shows entrances and exits. Emergency planners should advise law enforcement of the location of safes, vaults, cash, and especially valuable material and equipment and should provide telephone numbers for key management personnel.

Normal physical security features, such as fences and walls, may be destroyed or damaged in an emergency. Looting by employees and outsiders is a hazard that must be considered because spectators are attracted to any disaster scene. Hence, additional security personnel may be needed to maintain security and protect the assets and personnel of the organization. It is important not to involve all security personnel in disaster or fire control activities so that a sufficient number of them can continue to protect assets and personnel.

Personnel control is difficult, regardless of the number of employees assigned to perform security duties. Badges or passes to identify employees and others authorized in the area may be helpful. Simple arm bands can be issued quickly to auxiliary emergency staff (ASIS, 2003, 2004; FEMA, 1993; OSHA, 2004).

1.7.8 ALERT AND WARNING SYSTEM

The emergency plan should provide a method of warning those occupying the facility when an emergency exists. The method used should be sufficient to alert individuals as quickly as possible so that appropriate action can be taken (for instance, evacuating an area of the facility). Many local building or fire and safety codes require emergency warning and communications systems in high rises and other specified types of structures.

Ambient noise and distances must be considered in planning a warning system. Outdoor as well as indoor warning systems must be provided because individuals might be outdoors during an emergency. Existing communication systems—a public address system or the telephone system—may be used for indoor warnings.

Outdoor warning systems may use bells, whistles, sirens, or public address systems. A visual signal, such as a flashing light, might be used indoors as well as outdoors where noise prevents effective audible warning. Planners in the United States whose organizations are covered by the Americans with Disabilities Act may need to design warning systems that meet various placement, visibility, and audibility requirements.

All those occupying the facility should know what the warning signals are and what actions they must take when a warning is given. The warning system should be tested periodically when employees are in the facility so they can experience and become familiar with the warning (ASIS, 2003, 2004, 2005, 2009; FEMA, 1993; NFPA, 2010; NOD, 2009a; OSHA, 2001, 2004).

- Where are the primary exits?
- Where are the alternate exits?
- Will employees use the same exits for emergencies other than fires?
- How will the employer notify occupants to evacuate in an emergency other than a fire?
- How will the employer evacuate individuals with disabilities who require assistance?
- Where will the employer evacuate occupants for a short-term emergency (less than one hour)?
- Where are the alternate short-term evacuation areas?
- What will the employer do if the evacuation lasts for an extended period (more than one hour)?
- Where are the alternate extended evacuation areas?
- What will the employer do in the event of inclement weather for either a short-term or an extended evacuation?
- How will the employer account for employees, contractors, vendors, and visitors after an evacuation?
- Who will keep evacuees informed of the status of the incident?
- How will the employer transport occupants to a temporary evacuation area if it is not easily reached on foot?
- What will the employer do if occupants' personal vehicles or company vehicles are inside the security perimeter and therefore inaccessible?

Prepared by David H. Gilmore, CPP. Used with permission.

Figure 1-3
Evacuation Planning Questions

1.7.9 **EMERGENCY EVACUATION AND SHELTER-IN-PLACE**

In planning for an emergency that might entail a partial or full evacuation, such as a fire, hazmat spill, or bomb incident, planners need to think well beyond simply sounding an alarm and asking the building occupants to move to the nearest emergency exit. Figure 1-3 provides some of the questions that need to be considered in this aspect of emergency planning. For present purposes, short-term is less than one hour and extended is more than one hour. After about one hour, if not before, employees standing or sitting at an evacuation assembly point, particularly one outdoors, are likely to become restless and seek some kind of resolution.

In evacuation planning, organizations must consider alternate exits, routes, and assembly points. Furthermore, use of these alternates must be practiced regularly. One way to do so is to block the primary exit for a different floor or part of a building for each fire drill. This can be done with a sign reading "exit blocked due to smoke" or "exit blocked due to fire" or by having a monitor positioned at the exit to tell evacuees that it is not available. This forces evacuees to use alternate exits. Only through practice will people know what to do when the primary exit is blocked.

In multi-story buildings, in which employees typically depend on elevators to move between floors, the use of any fire stairs, whether primary or alternate, will be a new experience for some employees. This again points to the need for regular drills.

If, in the event of a fire, employees move across the street, down the block, or to the far end of the parking lot, then that is exactly what they should do in a drill, and the evacuation drill should continue until all occupants have reached the designated assembly points. The same rationale applies in a test of an organization's bomb incident or hazmat plan. The actual evacuation distances, which are likely to be considerably greater than those used in a fire, should be adhered to in conducting all drills.

Emergency plans should also provide for shelter-in-place for situations where evacuation is infeasible or undesirable, such as a hazmat release, tornado, or earthquake. Planners should carefully consider space requirements, sanitary arrangements, and provisions for food, water, and lodging when they select shelter areas. Planners should also consult with local authorities and the local Red Cross chapter to determine whether community shelters are already in place (ASIS, 2003, 2004, 2009; Broder, 2006; FEMA, 1993, 2004; NFPA, 2010; NOD, 2009a; OSHA, 2001, 2004).

1.7.10 **EMERGENCY SHUTDOWN AND RESTORATION**

The emergency plan should assign specific responsibility for equipment shutdown. The actual shutdown should be assigned to people familiar with the process. Shutdown of some equipment may take several hours, but a flood, fire, explosion, or earthquake may not give that much warning. Shutdown crews may be the last to leave the facility when evacuation is ordered, and they may even have to stay in the facility.

In such cases, maximum protection should be planned for shutdown crews, including a shelter that gives good assurance of survival. Crews should be kept as small as possible and drilled in fast shutdown procedures. Careful shutdown procedures greatly speed the recovery operation.

Restoration procedures should also be included in the emergency plan. If restoration has been planned, recovery is less difficult and more efficient. Developing a list of key recovery items simplifies emergency operations.

Efforts should not be wasted on areas or equipment that cannot be saved. It is better to concentrate efforts and save something than to spread the forces too thin and lose everything.

This is sometimes a painful decision, but it must be made. A pre-emergency review with managers and supervisors of the various physical assets within an area can help establish a salvage priority scheme.

The procurement or replacement cost of key assets should be evaluated, as should the cost impacts of the absence of those assets when attempting to restore normal operations.

The emergency plan should give priority to the facility structure after the emergency. The facility engineering crew should survey the building and grounds, particularly the building structure. At least one crew member should be technically competent to recognize structural weaknesses (ASIS, 2003, 2004; Broder, 2006; FEMA, 1993).

1.7.11 **RESOURCES AND LOGISTICS**

Depending on the nature of the incident and the type of organization, equipment and other logistical support may be provided in a number of different ways. Organizations may have some equipment that is set aside for emergency use only and other equipment that is in regular use but also designated for use in emergencies. Other equipment may need to be procured either from pre-identified commercial sources or from other organizations through mutual aid or interagency support arrangements.

Responsibility for the control of vehicles used during an emergency should be assigned to an individual with a designated alternate. All the organization's vehicles should be inventoried and included in the emergency plan.

Advance arrangements might be made to obtain additional vehicles from leasing companies or garages. Also, the use of employees' own vehicles might be included in the plan and arrangements made to pay for their use. In an emergency, vehicles may be needed to haul supplies and debris, to transport personnel, and to carry out rescue operations (ASIS, 2003, 2004, 2005, 2009; Broder, 2006; FEMA, 1993; NFPA, 2010).

Figure 1-4 indicates some key questions that need to be addressed when planning for logistical support, particularly for equipment and services that must be procured from outside the organization.

- What equipment or services are required?
- In what quantity?
- In what time frame?
- For how long?
- What sources are available?
- Can the source provide required support at all times?
- How long will it take the source to respond?
- How much will it cost?
- How is the source contacted during normal hours?
- How is the source contacted during other hours?
- Will the source transport equipment to the user?
- If not, how will it get to the user?
- Who will maintain or repair leased equipment?
- Who has authority for emergency procurement/lease?
- What documentation is required?
- How often will the source list be reviewed/verified?

Prepared by David H. Gilmore, CPP. Used with permission.

Figure 1-4
Resource and Logistics Questions

1.8 BUSINESS CONTINUITY, ORGANIZATIONAL RESILIENCE, AND CONTINUITY OF OPERATIONS (COOP)

Business continuity is defined by ASIS (2005) as

> a comprehensive managed effort to prioritize key business processes, identify significant threats to normal operation, and plan mitigation strategies to ensure effective and efficient organizational response to the challenges that surface during and after a crisis.

Another important concept, which can be applied to both public- and private-sector organizations, is organizational resilience, which is "the adaptive capacity of an organization in a complex and changing environment" (ASIS, 2009). In addition, resilience is (ASIS, 2009)

> the ability of an organization to resist being affected by an event or the ability to return to an acceptable level of performance in an acceptable period of time after being affected by an event.

A management system for organizational resilience is set forth in an American National Standard developed by ASIS (2009).

As indicated earlier, business continuity plans and continuity of operations plans should not be part of the organization's emergency operations plan but should be maintained as separate plans.

Depending on the nature and needs of the business, business continuity strategies may include resumption and recovery in place, the contracting out of selected functions, or relocation of critical functions and personnel to one or more sites (which may be controlled by the company or contracted from external sources). Whatever strategies are employed, the objective is to resume critical functions as quickly as possible and to restore the business to its pre-emergency condition and location or, if that is not possible, as in the case of the September 11, 2001, terrorist attacks on the World Trade Center towers, to a new location or level of operations.

A business impact analysis (BIA) is an integral part of the business continuity planning process. It is used to identify an entity's critical functions, to assess the impact of a disaster or other emergency on those functions over time, to determine the other elements of the business on which those critical functions depend, and to help develop and prioritize recovery strategies. Some references consider the BIA to be hazard neutral; in other words, it does not matter what caused the outage or disruption. Other references incorporate a hazard analysis as part of the BIA. Discussions of the BIA process can be found in several sources, such as ASIS (2005, 2009, 2010), Broder (2006), and NFPA (2010). Testing the business continuity (BC) plan is just as important as testing the emergency operations plan. A realistic functional test in a controlled environment is the best way to achieve this.

The BC or COOP plan should list the location of the alternate headquarters and operating locations and define who should report to them and under what conditions. Reporting centers might also be arranged so employees can signify their availability for work.

Communications necessary to maintain operations should be considered in establishing emergency operating sites. Options include radios (including citizens' band), cellular telephones, satellite telephone, and pagers.

Arrangements for storing vital backup records should be integrated into BC and COOP planning. Vital records are those that are necessary to ensure the survival of a business. To avoid what has been described as organizational amnesia, records considered essential for the resumption or continuation of operations may be stored at the emergency headquarters. Figure 1-5 lists some key business records. Government agencies should tailor the list to their particular requirements. The media in which records are maintained are less important than ensuring that sufficient retrieval equipment is available. Many organizations use distributed data processing methods, so much of the vital data may already be available at multiple locations.

accounts payable	incorporation certificates	plan: floor, building, etc.
accounts receivable	insurance policies	purchase orders
audits	inventory lists	receipt of payment
bank deposit data	leases	sales data
capital assets list	legal documents	service records and manuals,
charters and franchises	licenses	machinery
constitutions and bylaws	*manufacturing process data	social security receipts
contracts	minutes of directors' meetings	special correspondence
*customer data	notes receivable	statistical and operation data
debentures and bonds	patent and copyright authorizations	stock certificates
*engineering data	*payroll and personnel data policy	stock transfer books
general ledgers	manuals	stockholder lists
	pension data	tax records
*Indispensable for resumption of any level of normal activity.		

Figure 1-5

Examples of Vital Records

Planners should make arrangements for emergency funds at alternate operating sites. The funds should be sufficient to ensure the organization's ability to get back into operation without delay. In addition, lines of credit and means of obtaining additional funds should be arranged in advance (ASIS, 2003, 2004, 2005, 2009; Broder, 2006; FEMA, 1993; MSU, 2000; NFPA, 2010).

Key questions to consider in developing BC and COOP plans are shown in Figure 1-6.

- What functions are most critical?
- What will be required to restore those functions?
- What will be required to restore functions that are not time-sensitive?
- What conditions will necessitate a relocation?
- Who can order a relocation?
- What personnel or functions will be relocated?
- Where will they be relocated?
- At what point will a long-term relocation facility be required?
- Is the basic load of necessary equipment stored in portable containers for rapid deployment?
- Does the relocation facility have provisions for the following, as appropriate?

▪ Briefings and conferences	▪ Food service
▪ Communications	▪ Furniture
▪ Computer support	▪ Parking
▪ Copiers	▪ Recording equipment
▪ Emergency lodging	▪ Sanitary facilities
▪ Emergency power	▪ Security
▪ Facsimile machines	

Prepared by David H. Gilmore, CPP. Used with permission.

Figure 1-6
Continuity of Operations Planning Questions

1.9 FUTURE OF EMERGENCY MANAGEMENT

Given the ongoing presence of a wide array of natural and accidental threats—and the expanding array of terrorist threats that confront modern society—emergency management will continue to be a vital function in both the public and private sectors. As new threats and vulnerabilities are identified, emergency managers will need to adapt their plans, programs, and procedures accordingly. As the threats with which society is confronted evolve, so must emergency management.

REFERENCES

ASIS International. (2003). *Emergency planning handbook* (2d ed.) Alexandria, VA: ASIS International.

ASIS International. (2004). *Manual de planificación de emergencias (*Segunda edición). Alexandria, VA: ASIS International.

ASIS International. (2005). *Business continuity guideline: A practical approach for emergency preparedness, crisis management, and disaster recovery.* Alexandria, VA: ASIS International.

ASIS International. (2009). *Organizational resilience: Security, preparedness and continuity management systems—Requirements with guidance for use.* American National Standard ASIS SPC.1-2009. Alexandria, VA: ASIS International.

ASIS International and British Standards Institution, Inc. (2010). *Business continuity management systems: Requirements with guidance for use.* American National Standard ASIS/BSI BCM.01-2010. Alexandria, VA: ASIS International.

Broder, J. F., CPP. (2006). *Risk analysis and the security survey* (3rd ed.). Burlington, MA: Elsevier/Butterworth-Heinemann.

Federal Emergency Management Agency. (1993). *Emergency management guide for business and industry.* FEMA Publication 141.Washington, DC: Federal Emergency Management Agency.

Federal Emergency Management Agency. (2007a). *National incident management system.* FEMA Publication 501. Washington, DC: Federal Emergency Management Agency. Available: http://www.fema.gov/pdf/emergency/nrf/nrf-nims.pdf [2011, August 16].

Federal Emergency Management Agency. (2007b). *National Incident Management System Resource Center: Glossary.* Washington, DC. Federal Emergency Management Agency. Available: http://www.fema.gov/emergency/nims/Glossary.shtm [2011, August 16].

Federal Emergency Management Agency. (2010a). *Comprehensive planning guide: A guide for all-hazard emergency operations planning.* FEMA Publication CPG 101, Version 2.0. Washington, DC: Federal Emergency Management Agency.

Federal Emergency Management Agency. (2010b). *Guidance on planning for integration of functional needs support services in general population shelters.* Washington, DC: Federal Emergency Management Agency.

Michigan State University School of Criminal Justice. (2000). *Critical incident protocol: A public and private partnership.* East Lansing, MI: Michigan State University.

National Fire Protection Association. (2010). *Standard on disaster/emergency management and business continuity programs.* NFPA 1600. Quincy, MA: National Fire Protection Association.

National Organization on Disability. (2009a). *Functional needs of people with disabilities: Guide for emergency planners, managers, and responders* (Revised ed.). Washington, DC: National Organization on Disability.

National Organization on Disability. (2009b). Prepare yourself: Disaster readiness tips for people with disabilities. Washington, DC: National Organization on Disability.

Occupational Safety and Health Administration, U.S. Department of Labor. (2001). *How to prepare for workplace emergencies and evacuations.* OSHA Publication 3088 (revised). Washington, DC: Occupational Safety and Health Administration.

Occupational Safety and Health Administration, U.S. Department of Labor. (2004). *Principal emergency response and preparedness: Requirements and guidance.* OSHA Publication 312206R. Washington, DC: Occupational Safety and Health Administration.

U.S. Department of Homeland Security. (2008). *National incident management system.* Washington, DC: U.S. Department of Homeland Security. Available: http://www.fema.gov/pdf/emergency/nims/NIMS_core.pdf [2011, August 16].

U.S. Department of Homeland Security. (n.d.) National response framework (NRF)—Fact sheet. Washington, DC. U.S. Department of Homeland Security. Available: http://www.fema.gov/pdf/emergency/nrf/NRFOnePageFactSheet.pdf [2011, August 16].

CHAPTER 2
TERRORISM AFFECTING THE GLOBAL WORKPLACE

2.1 HISTORY OF TERROR

2.1.1 THE OLD TERRORISTS

Terrorism has been practiced for millennia. One can see the emergence of terrorism in the actions of many groups throughout history:

- Jewish Zealots fighting Roman occupation of Israel in the first century A.D.

- Indian Thuggees of the seventh century

- Muslim Assassins of the 11th and 12th centuries

- French revolutionaries of the 18th century

These terrorists have political motivations; use violence as a didactic tool; are organized, deliberate, and systematic in their attacks; often attack targets that symbolize the state; desire attention, not a large body count; enjoy revolutionary connotations; cloak themselves in military jargon; and generally describe themselves as freedom fighters, liberators, ethnic self-defense movements, or executors of righteous vengeance.

These groups have traditional motivations. Their strategies and tactics remain similar to those observed for centuries. The groups generally show some discretion and moderation in both their selection of targets (still largely symbolic) and their means of attack. Their organizational structures remain predictable, if still difficult to penetrate using technical or human intelligence.

2.1.2 **THE NEW TERRORISTS**

The emerging new terrorist type is at once broader and more amorphous. The motivations of these new terrorists include religious fanaticism, supremacist ideology, or apocalyptic prophecy. The new terrorists have overcome the obstacles to using weapons of mass destruction (WMDs), such as chemical, biological, and radiological weapons.

Terrorists of the radical right, some of whom identify themselves as Christian, have formed a dangerous addition to the list of terrorists. Racist, ethnically exclusive, anti-government, and with the power of righteousness behind them, these new terrorists are little constrained when compared to their old, leftist terrorist peers. Their use of violence is less constrained and less didactic. They may attack targets purely for shock value, not satisfied to strike only at symbolic targets. These terrorists may have smaller constituencies, or their constituencies may be closed. They may be led by charismatic persons who are able to manipulate the actions of the whole.

The face of terrorism changed on September 11, 2001. Earlier terrorism encompassed assassinations, kidnappings, and suicidal individuals who killed others with explosives and died in the process. Trucks filled with explosives had been used to demolish government buildings, causing hundreds of casualties, as was done in Oklahoma City. However, the act of deliberately crashing a civilian aircraft and passengers into a public building was unprecedented. In addition, the anthrax contamination of U.S. postal facilities, government offices, and commercial buildings shortly after September 11 brought another facet of terrorism to world attention.

Of course, the effects of the 9/11 attacks were graphically displayed in the media. The author of *Mass-Mediated Terrorism* (Nacos, 2002) notes that although the term "media terrorism" captures terrorists' emphasis on communicating their deeds and causes, the expression could be misunderstood to suggest a compliant role on the part of the media. She thus calls terrorists' use of the media "mass-mediated terrorism." She contends that terrorists vie for publicity by exploiting far-reaching, instant, global media networks to spread news of their violence. Nacos also documents how terrorist networks have become a convenient tool for recruiting followers and soliciting donations. Specifically, she paints a picture of the Internet as a forum for communication and promotion for "apostles of hate." Nacos makes the case that terrorist incidents are as much "infotainment" as hard news. Infotainment, she notes, thrives on the very themes that terrorism offers: tragedy, shock, anger, grief, fear, and panic. These are the ideal ingredients for transforming real-life terror into breathtaking thrillers or heartbreaking soap operas designed to captivate and stir up audiences.

Still, Nacos writes that 9/11 brought Americans and the press closer together than during normal times or even previous crises (such as the first Gulf War). Accounting for this change of heart, Nacos says, was "the public's appreciation of the flow of information from the media, gratitude for the media's communication of important information to the public, and relief at not having to watch (or, at least, less frequently watch) the media chase after survivors and relatives of victims." Coverage of the events overshadowed other news for months. Many other terrorist attacks, though smaller, were carried out in relative obscurity during that period.

As for the United States, terrorism is defined in the *Code of Federal Regulations* (28 CFR 0.85) as

> the unlawful use of force and violence against persons or property to intimidate or coerce a government, the civilian population, or any segment thereof, in furtherance of political or social objectives.

The FBI further describes terrorism as either domestic or international, depending on the origin, base, and objectives of the terrorist organization. The FBI uses the following definitions of terrorism:

- **Domestic terrorism** refers to activities that involve acts dangerous to human life that are a violation of the criminal laws of the United States or of any state; appear to be intended to intimidate or coerce a civilian population [or] to influence the policy of a government by mass destruction, assassination, or kidnapping; and occur primarily within the territorial jurisdiction of the United States (18 USC § 2331(5)).

- **International terrorism** involves violent acts or acts dangerous to human life that are a violation of the criminal laws of the United States or any state, or that would be a criminal violation if committed within the jurisdiction of the United States or any state. These acts appear to be intended to intimidate or coerce a civilian population; influence the policy of a government by intimidation or coercion; or affect the conduct of a government by mass destruction, assassination, or kidnapping; and occur primarily outside the territorial jurisdiction of the United States or transcend national boundaries in terms of the means by which they are accomplished, the persons they appear intended to intimidate or coerce, or the locale in which their perpetrators operate or seek asylum (18 USC § 2331(1)).

In Canada, the 2001 Anti-Terrorism Act defines terrorist activity as an action that takes place either within or outside Canada that

> is an offence under any one of ten listed UN counter-terrorism conventions and protocols; or, is taken for political, religious or ideological purposes and intimidates the public concerning its security, or compels a government to do something (or not do something), by intentionally killing, seriously harming or endangering a person, causing substantial property damage that is likely to seriously harm people or by seriously interfering with or disrupting an essential service, facility or system.

2.2 APPROACHES TO TERRORISM ANALYSIS

The possibility of serious personal harm or death arouses powerful emotions. It is the exploitation of such emotions that allows terrorist threats to succeed. The real targets of terrorist violence are not always the actual victims, but rather the intended audience. For example, a hijacked plane sends a message to a government, which is often the intended target. The objective of terrorism is not usually just to kill people. It is a violence campaign designed to create an atmosphere of fear and alarm and thereby gain attention. The violence carried out by most terrorist groups is intended to shock. Hence, they frequently choose innocent civilians as targets.

2.2.1 MULTICAUSAL APPROACH

Terrorism usually results from several causes at once—psychological, economic, political, religious, sociological, and even physiological. Moreover, the causes of revolution and political violence in general are also the causes of terrorism. These include ethnic conflicts, religious and ideological conflicts, poverty, modernization stresses, political inequities, lack of peaceful communication channels, traditions of violence, the existence of a revolutionary group, governmental weakness and ineptitude, erosions of confidence in a regime, and deep divisions within governing elites and leadership groups.

2.2.2 POLITICAL APPROACH

Environments conducive to the rise of terrorism include international and national environments, as well as universities, where many terrorists first become familiar with Marxist-Leninist ideology or other revolutionary ideas and get involved with radical groups. Analysts may distinguish between precipitants that start an outbreak of violence and preconditions that allow the precipitants to instigate the action. Political scientists have further subdivided preconditions into permissive factors, which engender a terrorist strategy and make it attractive to political dissidents, and direct situational factors, which motivate terrorists. Permissive causes include urbanization, the transportation system (for example, by allowing a terrorist to escape quickly to another country by taking a flight), communications media, weapons availability, and the absence of security measures. An example of a situational factor for Palestinians would be the loss of their homeland.

2.2.3 ORGANIZATIONAL APPROACH

Some analysts see terrorism as a rational, strategic course of action decided on by a group. That interpretation would not apply to all terrorist organizations, but it may correctly describe guerilla groups organized along traditional Marxist-Leninist lines. In the Revolutionary Armed Forces of Colombia (FARC), for example, the six members of a general secretariat participate in decision making under the leadership of a secretary general. By contrast, bona fide terrorist groups, like cults, are often totally dominated by a single leader, such as Osama bin Laden, Shoko Asahara, or the Abu Nidal. It seems improbable that such dominating leaders would make their decisions through a group vote. By most accounts, established terrorist leaders give instructions to hijack a jetliner, assassinate a particular person, bomb a U.S. embassy, and so forth but leave operational details to their lieutenants.

2.2.4 PSYCHOLOGICAL APPROACH

The psychological approach examines terrorists' recruitment, personalities, beliefs, attitudes, motivations, and careers as terrorists. Groups that make universal appeals in the name of brotherhood, economic justice, or religion are not constrained by fears of alienating world opinion but, rather, place themselves above it.

The world's extremists are becoming increasingly dangerous. The most dangerous threat today comes from the global jihadist movement. Kepel's book *The War for Muslim Minds: Islam and the West* (2004) states that the battle for Muslim minds during the next decade "will be fought in the communities of believers on the outskirts of London, Paris, and other European cities, where Islam is already a growing part of the West." In *The Crisis of Islam: Holy War and Unholy Terror,* Bernard Lewis (2004) provides a realistic and disturbing assessment of the greatest threat to civilized life.

According to Kohlmann (2004), the young men who went to Afghanistan from Saudi Arabia, Egypt, Algeria, Yemen, and elsewhere to free Afghanistan from the Soviets are revered to this day as heroes. These inexperienced but unusually persistent fighters referred to themselves as mujahideen (meaning strugglers or holy warriors). The struggle caught the imagination of the Islamic world. Notions of universal Muslim brotherhood were awakened. A number of Arab and Islamic states rallied to the cause, arranging for money and weapons for the mujahideen.

2.3 WINNING THE WAR ON TERRORISM

In the global war on terrorism, lack of cooperation has plagued law enforcement and intelligence work. Those with the responsibility for protection strategies must use an all-hazards approach wherein countermeasures are multifaceted. In *Defending the Homeland: Domestic Intelligence, Law Enforcement, and Security*, Jonathan White (2004) provides useful insights into the troubles between the intelligence community and the law enforcement community. He also explores the advantages and disadvantages of the Patriot Act and recommends means whereby the intelligence community can work with law enforcement.

To many, the war on terrorism is in faraway places, yet security professionals know it is very near. In the book *Imperial Hubris: Why the West is Losing the War on Terror* (2004), written by an unnamed counterterrorism expert, the author states, "We are losing the war on terror." He continues, "What's needed is for the West to proceed with relentless, brutal, and, yes, blood-soaked offensive military actions until we have annihilated the Islamists who threaten us." The author adds this observation:

> The ferocious, militaristic, and bin Laden-echoing content of many of the fatwas calling for a defensive jihad against the United States because of its invasion of Iraq shows that Islamic scholars across the theological spectrum share many of bin Laden's perceptions of U.S. policy. Hence, the fatwas have urged people to embark on the path of jihad… It is impossible to understand the threat America faces until the intensity and pervasiveness of this hatred is recognized.

Another source that examines the threat posed by the global jihadist movement is *The Age of Sacred Terror: Radical Islam's War Against America* (Benjamin and Simon, 2003). It provides an analysis of radical terrorism, complemented by a rich knowledge base about al Qaeda's adherence to the teachings of ibn Taymiyya, a medieval Muslim theologian. The authors explore how radical preachers turn alienation and newly acquired religious commitment into hate.

Although many people focus on al Qaeda as the primary terrorist threat, the global jihadist movement comprises many groups and individuals apart from al Qaeda. Rashid (2002) focuses on Kazakhstan, Tajikistan, Uzbekistan, Kyrgyzstan, and Turkmenistan. In *Jihad: The Rise of Militant Islam in Central Asia*, Rashid describes the conflicts between Islamic militants and the governments of those countries, showing how crises within those states have increased. In addition, Rashid suggests that the region's most influential militant groups are the Uighur Islamic militants (who are waging a guerrilla war against Chinese authorities), the Islamic Movement of Uzbekistan (IMU), and the Hizb ut-Tahrir (HT). The IMU has been affiliated with the Taliban and Osama bin Laden, and the HT has spread leaflets criticizing the United States and resists U.S. occupation of Muslim soil.

Rashid describes Muhammad's teachings about jihad and discusses jihadi groups' obsession with implementing sharia (Islamic law). Rashid characterizes the Taliban and al Qaeda as cults that strip Islam of its values, humanism, and spirituality. He claims that by refusing to accommodate traditional Islam, democracy, and interethnic harmony, the Central Asian governments fuel the fires of extremism. In addition, he claims that the main reason for the explosion of Islamic militancy today is Russian repression. The more the Russians tried to stamp out Islam, the more it spread throughout Central Asia as an act of ethnic, regional, and religious resistance.

2.4 STATE-SPONSORED TERRORISM

Over the years, terrorism has become more widespread as indigenous groups with long-standing causes adopt terrorist techniques. In addition, a number of modern states continue to secretly—and sometimes openly—sponsor terrorist movements in furtherance of their political aims. Transnational terrorism—terrorist activity across national borders—has continued steadily.

The following section summarizes the U.S. Department of State's characterization of "state sponsors of terror" (U.S. Department of State, 2005). In general, the State Department report observes that Iraq, as it transitioned to democracy, ceased to support terrorism. As a result, its designation as a state sponsor of terrorism was rescinded in October 2004. Libya and Sudan took significant steps to cooperate in the global war on terrorism in 2004. Cuba, Iran, North Korea, and Syria, however, continued to maintain their ties to terrorism. These countries provide a critical foundation for terrorist groups. Without state sponsors, terrorist groups would have a much more difficult time obtaining the funds, weapons, materials, and secure areas they require to plan and conduct operations. Most worrisome is that these countries also have the capabilities to manufacture weapons of mass destruction and other destabilizing technologies that could fall into the hands of terrorists.

2.5 COUNTERTERRORISM EFFORTS

Before 9/11/01, police and counterintelligence agencies throughout the world were already cooperating to fight terrorism, but after that date the cooperative effort intensified. The original eight countries that formed the main cooperative effort include the United States, Canada, France, Germany, Italy, Japan, Russia, and the United Kingdom. The countries promote international standards for airport security, explosives detection, and vehicle identification while exchanging information on terrorist organizations. Such cooperation has proved that modern intelligence and police methods, together with a sharing of sensitive information between governments, can result in an effective counterterrorism program.

Terrorism presents a constantly changing panorama. Any threat assessment program should include regularly updated reports to reflect the latest information on terrorist groups, their modus operandi, and targeting strategies. Although companies are reluctant to release details of a terrorist incident because the appearance of success may spread, threat assessments and updated information can be obtained from government agencies in many countries, as well as from private sources, responsible publications, and research organizations.

A convenient source of current information is the U.S. Department of State, which maintains regularly updated summaries of significant terrorist groups operating throughout the world. Information for overseas business travel is also available. Travel warnings are available at http://travel.state.gov/travel/cis_pa_tw/tw/tw_1764.html. A traveler's hot line may be accessed at (202) 647–5225.

2.6 CHEMICAL, BIOLOGICAL, RADIOLOGICAL, AND NUCLEAR (CBRN) TERRORISM

In 2003, U.S. President George W. Bush, European Council President Konstantinos Simitis, and European Commission President Romano Prodi said the following in a joint statement (Joint Statement on Proliferation, 2003):

> Production of weapons of mass destruction (WMD) and their delivery systems constitutes a major threat to international peace and security. The threat is compounded by the interests of terrorists in acquiring WMD. This would undermine the foundations of international order. We pledge to use all means available to avert WMD proliferation and the calamities that would follow.

Terrorist groups—including al Qaeda—are increasingly looking to chemical, biological, radiological, and nuclear (CBRN) materials as a means to cause mass casualties rivaling or exceeding those of September 11, 2001. Significant amounts of CBRN materials and information remain available to terrorists. Osama bin Laden said that acquiring WMD is a duty, and he threatened to use such weapons. This rhetoric was underscored by reports that documents retrieved from al Qaeda facilities in Afghanistan contain information on CBRN materials. The threat is not limited to al Qaeda. Small but growing numbers of other terrorist groups are also interested in CBRN materials. In France in 2002, police seized a chemical contamination suit and arrested members of a terrorist cell that allegedly was planning an attack using chemical agents.

To date, CBRN terrorism has generally involved improvised delivery means that have been only marginally effective. Moreover, aside from the 1995 Aum Shinrikyo attacks in Tokyo and the 2001 U.S. anthrax attacks, the materials employed have been crudely manufactured. Other events have involved dual-use materials that have legitimate civilian applications, such as industrial chemicals, poisons, pesticides, and radiological materials embedded in measuring instruments. Although terrorist attacks using such materials and delivery systems can cause significant casualties and damage, such events pale in comparison to the casualties and damage that could occur if terrorists acquired WMDs and the ability to deliver them effectively. Preventing the proliferation of WMDs, their delivery systems, and related materials and technologies has long been a pillar of national security. Since September 11, the nonproliferation of WMDs has become even more urgent. President Bush made this clear in his December 2002 National Strategy to Combat Weapons of Mass Destruction, in which he set out a comprehensive strategy to prevent WMD proliferation.

In May 2003, President Bush announced the Proliferation Security Initiative (PSI), a global multilateral arrangement to seize sensitive cargo. PSI participants jointly explore and train in the best use of counterproliferation tools—diplomatic, intelligence, and operational. The United States promotes more stringent nonproliferation policies and programs; strengthened export controls; and improved border security to prevent terrorists or their state sponsors from acquiring WMD, their delivery systems, related materials, or technologies.

Generally, bombings with conventional explosives are the principal form of terrorist activity, but the probability of future CBRN attacks is increasing. The use of sarin gas in the terrorist attack on Tokyo subway trains in 1995 and the 2001 anthrax incidents in the United States demonstrate the practicality of such agents.

A Faceless Enemy: The Origins of Modern Terrorism (Schweitzer & Schweitzer, 2002) discusses weapons that are readily available to terrorists and examines "superterrorism," which the authors define as "the committing of violent acts using advanced technological tools to cause massive damage to populations and/or to public and private support networks." The book describes the poor physical security surrounding nuclear and biochemical materials in states comprising the former Soviet Union. The authors claim that the United States has become home to hundreds and probably thousands of terrorists and has thus become a central node in their international networks.

Historically, weapons of mass destruction were thought of as nuclear weapons. Recent events have demonstrated the practical use of other weapons and systems as WMDs.

Chemical and biological weapons have been referred to as "the poor man's nuclear weapon" because those who cannot obtain nuclear weapons have pursued chemical and biological agents as a second best option. Most terrorists, thus far, have not had WMDs available to them.

Nuclear Terrorism: The Ultimate Preventable Catastrophe (Allison, 2004) offers a lucid explanation of special and general theories of nuclear terrorism. Allison points out what kind of devastation a nuclear explosion from a 10-kiloton weapon would have on specific cities, such as New York City, Chicago, and Boston: "From the epicenter of the blast to a distance of approximately a third of a mile, every structure and individual would vanish in a vaporous haze." He also describes the attractiveness of nuclear plants as terrorist targets. Such plants house spent fuel rods, which are stored in water to prevent the heat from their residual radioactivity from melting them. Should the fuel rods become ignited, the resulting fire would spew radioactivity into the environment in amounts that could reach three or four times the amount released in the Chernobyl accident.

Allison further states that 40,000 to 80,000 nuclear weapons may be in the former Soviet Union, poorly controlled and poorly stored. A chapter is devoted to discussing the potential of various terrorist groups to use WMDs. The use of such weapons in state-sponsored terrorism, by a nation or terrorist group, certainly lies in the realm of possibility.

2.7 CYBER WEAPONS

The vulnerability of critical infrastructures to a cyberattack is also readily apparent. These infrastructures—including telecommunications, energy, banking and finance, water systems, government operations, and emergency services—provide the foundation for a modern industrialized society. Businesses and governments have become more aware of the vulnerability of computerized systems to attack through the Internet.

Developing a CBRN weapon can be complex and involve a significant financial investment. It can be a dangerous undertaking with uncertain results. In contrast, the creator of the Love Bug virus toiled in a safe environment and caused billions of dollars in recovery costs and lost productivity with a single piece of malicious code.

The world relies increasingly on new information technologies and the Internet to conduct business, manage industrial activities, engage in personal communications, and perform scientific research. While these technologies allow for enormous gains in efficiency, productivity, and communications, they also create new vulnerabilities. They are both user-friendly and abuser-friendly. The same interconnectivity that makes it possible for legitimate users to transmit information around the globe at the click of a mouse also creates unprecedented opportunities for criminals, terrorists, and hostile governments.

Public and private records are now digitized, and many commercial and financial transactions depend fully on digitized communications over unsecure networks. Essential infrastructures—such as power grids, telecommunications systems, and air traffic control operations—have shifted from mechanical or electrical control to electronic control.

In the rush to more efficient operations, users have not paid sufficient attention to the risk of intentional disruption. As hacker intrusions and virus attacks have disrupted business and government operations, the threat has become more apparent.

After September 11, 2001, the threat of terrorist attacks on government and commercial networks crystallized dramatically. Exposure to cyberterrorism increases daily as commerce and industry increase their use of computerized systems. Particularly vulnerable are banking and finance systems; water supply systems; transportation systems; refineries and pipelines; radio and telephone communications systems; and electrical generation, transmission, and distribution systems. The exposures may lie in the complexity and interdependence of the systems themselves or in certain vulnerable portions of a system.

The disruption of vital utility, communications, or transportation systems would cause wide-spread alarm. Unconfirmed reports suggest that both military and commercial computer systems have been disrupted and extortion demands made to cease the disruptions.

Many businesses have responded to threats by installing hardware and software to thwart attacks on their systems. However, systems intended for large numbers of users—such as educational institutions—are particularly vulnerable to intrusion. These systems are usually linked to other systems for ease of use, and intruders move through several systems to hide the origin of an attack. New methods of attack are developed daily, and the process of vulnerability assessment must be continuous.

2.8 **CONVENTIONAL WEAPONS**

The ready supply of conventional weapons is obvious from the number of arsenals seized from street criminals and from media reports of factional struggles throughout the world. Automatic rifles and machine guns, rocket and grenade launchers, even surface-to-air missiles are already used by criminals and terrorists. Together with improvised and commercial explosives, these weapons make it possible for a small band of determined individuals to commence operations that, even if not ultimately successful, could wreak mass havoc.

Space technology and commercial electronics have been applied to the weapons of the infantryman. Thermodynamically efficient propellants and small, two-stage, solid-fuel propulsion systems have reduced the requirements for heavy gun barrels and increased the range of small projectiles. Improvements in metallurgy, plastic compounds, and glass fibers permit further reductions in the size and weight of firing tubes. New sighting and tracking devices and aerodynamic testing of projectile shapes have increased range and accuracy. Developments in explosive and shaped charges have added to the destructive power. The result is a new range of weapons that are smaller, lighter, more accurate at greater range, and more destructive than any weapons previously available.

The most dramatic development in individual weaponry is that of precision-guided munitions (PGMs) or man-portable air defense systems (MANPADS). Common PGMs have an effective range of one to three and a half kilometers, and some can penetrate up to two meters of concrete or more than half a meter of heavy armor. They are easy to operate—an advantage to groups whose members may not be trained—and highly destructive. They were originally designed to destroy tactical aircraft and tanks. A single missile can be used against both aircraft and tanks. MANPADS are munitions that can correct their course in flight so that accuracy approaches certainty. MANPADS are lightweight and usually can be carried and operated by one person.

2.9 SUMMARY

Terrorism, in all its forms, will be a continuing consideration for the assets protection professional. Bombing and kidnapping will continue to be the major activities of terrorist groups; however, the possibility of the use of nonconventional weapons cannot be discounted. Cyber terrorism may also increase. The number of terrorist incidents may continue to decline, but the number of casualties may rise with the use of larger explosive devices and nonconventional attacks. High-profile organizations and facilities, both governmental and civilian, will be the primary targets. Asymmetric attacks and multiple simultaneous attacks may be expected. The threat can be reduced by recognition of the problem, detailed threat assessment, intelligence gathering, and the patient application of multiple and sustained deterrent measures.

REFERENCES

Allison, G. (2004). *Nuclear terrorism: The ultimate preventable catastrophe*. New York, NY: Times Books.

Benjamin, D., & Simon, S. (2003). *The age of sacred terror: Radical Islam's war against America*. New York, NY: Random House.

Imperial hubris: Why the West is losing the war on terror. (2004). Dulles, VA: Brassey's, Inc.

Joint statement on proliferation of weapons of mass destruction by President George W. Bush, European Council President Konstandinos Simitis, and European Commission President Romano Prodi. (2003). Washington, DC: Office of the Press Secretary, The White House.

Kepel, G. (2004). *The war for Muslim minds: Islam and the West*. Cambridge, MA: Harvard University Press.

Kohlmann, E. (2004). *Al-Qaida's jihad in Europe: The Afghan-Bosnian network*. Oxford, United Kingdom: Berg Publishing.

Lewis, B. (2003). *The Crisis of Islam: Holy war and unholy terror*. New York, NY: Random House.

Nacos, B. (2002). *Mass-mediated terrorism: The central role of the media in terrorism and counterterrorism*. Lanham, MD: Rowman & Littlefield Publishers.

Rashid, A. (2002). *Jihad: The rise of militant Islam in Central Asia*. New York, NY: Penguin Putnam Inc.

Schweitzer, G., & Schweitzer, C. (2002). *A faceless enemy: The origins of modern terrorism*. Cambridge, MA: Perseus Publishing.

U.S. Department of State. (2005). *Country reports on terrorism 2004*. Washington, DC: U.S. Department of State. Available: www.state.gov/documents/organization/45313.pdf [2011, August 15].

White, J. R. (2004). *Defending the homeland: Domestic intelligence, law enforcement, and security*. Belmont, CA: Wadsworth/Thomson Learning.

ADDITIONAL SOURCES

A highly explosive mixture. (2001, October 22). *U.S. News & World Report*.

Albright, D., & Kramer, K. (2004, November/December). Fissile material: Stockpiles still growing. *Bulletin of the Atomic Scientists*, 14–15.

An outbreak of terror that dances on the head of a pin. (2001, October 29). *U.S. News & World Report*.

Anti-terrorism act. (2001). Government of Canada.

Beaudry, M. H. (2003). Terrorist morphology. *Counterterrorism Homeland Security Reports, 10*(3), 2–3.

Beckmann, G. (1999, January). Creating and maintaining security databases. *Security Technology & Design.*

Bremer, L. P., III. (2001, March). Assessing U.S. counterterrorism efforts. *Security Management.*

Central Intelligence Agency. (2002). *Unclassified report to Congress on the acquisition of technology relating to weapons of mass destruction and advanced conventional munitions.* Washington, DC: Central Intelligence Agency.

Cordesman, A. H. (2001). *If we fight Iraq: Iraq and its weapons of mass destruction.* Washington, DC: Center for Strategic and International Studies.

Cullison, A., & Higgins, A. (2002, August 2). Strained alliance: Inside al Qaeda's Afghan turmoil. *Wall Street Journal.*

Falkenrath, R., Newman, R., & Thayer, B. (1999). *America's Achilles heel: Nuclear, biological and chemical terrorism and covert attack.* Cambridge, MA: MIT Press.

Federal Emergency Management Agency. (2001). *Backgrounder: Terrorism.* Washington, DC: Federal Emergency Management Agency.

Federal Emergency Management Agency. (2001). *Guide for all-hazard emergency operations planning.* Attachment G—Terrorism, Chapter 6, State and Local Guide 101. Washington, DC: Federal Emergency Management Agency.

Gearty, C. (1997). *The future of terrorism.* London: Phoenix.

Germs of terror (2001, October 29). *U.S. News & World Report.*

Gertz, B. (2005, April 20). Reports reveal Zarqawi nuclear threat. *Washington Times*, p. 3.

Gingrich, N. (2001, April). Threats of mass disruption. *Information Security.*

Gips, M. (1997, November). Bioterrorism in our midst? *Security Management.*

Halperin, E. (1976). *Terrorism in Latin America.* Beverly Hills, CA: Sage Publications.

Hamit, F. (1999, June). Beating the bio-terror threat. *Security Technology & Design.*

Heathcote, M. S. R. (2002, May). How can terrorism risks be managed? *Security Management.*

Jaber, H. (1997). *Hezbollah: Born with a vengeance.* New York: Columbia University Press.

Jenkins, R. M. (1992, September). The Islamic connection. *Security Management.*

Johnson, L. C. (1997, April). The fall of terrorism. *Security Management.*

Kushner, H. W. (1996, June). Can security measures stop terrorism? *Security Management.*

Leader, S. H. (1997, April). The rise of terrorism. *Security Management.*

Middleton, B. (1999, February). Mapping a network security strategy. *Security Management.*

Mizell, L. R., Jr. (1998). *Target USA: The inside story of the new terrorist war.* New York, NY: John Wiley & Sons.

Morgan, R. (1989). *The demon lover: The roots of terrorism.* New York, NY: Simon & Schuster.

Nason, R. R. (2000, October). Threats for the new millennium. *Security Technology & Design.*

Neeley, D. (1998, December). How to keep out bad characters. *Security Management.*

Newman, G. *Understanding violence.* New York, NY: The Maple Press Company.

Next stop, Colombia. (2002, February 25). *U.S. News & World Report*, p. 23.

Ozier, W. (1999, January). Assessing a nation's risk. *Information Security.*

Piazza, P. (2002, May). Health alerts to fight bioterrorism. *Security Management.*

Propst, R. (2002). New terrorists, new attack means? Categorizing terrorist challenges for the early 21st century. Available: http://www.homelandsecurity.org/journal/articles/propstnewterrorist print.htm [2011, August 15].

Pillar, P. R. (2001, May). Is the terrorist threat misunderstood? *Security Management.*

Scott, M. W. (2004, May 18). Animal rights: Activism vs. criminality. Testimony before United States Senate Committee on the Judiciary. Washington, DC.

Smith, G. D. (1998). *Single issue terrorism.* Commentary No. 74, Canadian Security Intelligence Service.

Stanton, J. J. (2000, August). Is the country ready for cyberwarfare? *Security Management.*

Stedman, M. J. (2000, April). Cyber-terrorism: The end of the world as we know it. *Security Technology & Design.*

Stedman, M. J. (2000, September). Cyberwarfare warnings point to ominous U.S. info security lapse. *Security Technology & Design.*

Terrorism at the mall? (1997, December). *Security Management.*

The joy of the Turks; the fury of the Kurds. (1999, March 1). *U.S. News & World Report.*

U.S. Department of State. (2002). *Patterns of Global Terrorism: 2001.* Washington, DC: U.S. Department of State.

U.S. Department of State (2005). Foreign terrorist organizations. Fact sheet. Office of Counterterrorism. Washington, DC: U.S. Department of State.

Wiles, J. (1999, January). High tech crime: A new type of disaster. *Security Technology & Design.*

CHAPTER 3
BOMB INCIDENT MANAGEMENT

3.1 INTRODUCTION TO BOMB INCIDENTS

Security managers can develop and implement protective measures to protect people, information, and capabilities from bombs. One might think it is preferable to evacuate in all cases (better safe than sorry), but organizations must be able to continue operating until it is determined that a hazard probably exists and that there is a legitimate need to evacuate all or part of the site. This document provides guidance on developing appropriate bomb safety and security measures to protect operations and profitability as well as life and property.

Bomb incidents pose considerable challenges to security managers. The use or threat of bombs supports a wide range of political, criminal, and social motives. A bomb threat takes few resources but may cause considerable disruption. All assets can be considered vulnerable to an explosion. In many countries, explosives are readily available; where they are not, explosive and incendiary compounds can be made from household and industrial materials. A further challenge is that the bomber chooses the motive, target, placement, concealment, activation method, and timing of the attack. Moreover, the bomber usually does not need to be at the scene during the explosion. In addition, bomb incidents are newsworthy.

Bomb security builds on common security principles such as access control, defense-in-depth, security awareness training, business continuity, emergency management, and human resource support for victims. Bomb response is a management-level responsibility, requiring the ability to make decisions quickly and with limited information. An effective bomb incident management capability requires procedures that are relevant to the organization and based on sound security analysis. How an organization manages a bomb incident can affect its reputation and even determine its survival, including its ability to defend itself in court.

Bombings have been used by criminals and political activists for centuries. Bombs are literally devastating with large amounts of energy released in milliseconds, creating forces capable of destroying buildings, information technology (IT) systems, vehicles, and equipment and killing and injuring staff, clients, and the public. The effects of a bomb may be similar to those of an industrial accident or natural disaster but are caused by deliberate human action. Even the threat of a bomb can cause fear and disruption.

An explosion's blast wave and fragmentation may injure or kill people in the immediate vicinity; items near the explosion will be damaged, resulting in projected fragments; ceiling tiles will be dislodged, adding to the damage and making movement and observation difficult; glass partitions and windows may shatter, creating glass fragments; smoke may develop; and fire sprinklers may be damaged, adding water to the scene. In addition, nearby cabling, piping, and junctions may be damaged, causing problems with power, fire-fighting systems, sewerage, communications, and IT. The building fabric, too, may be weakened.

After the explosion, the site will be a complex crime scene. If a fatality has occurred, investigators may isolate the area for weeks while they sift through the evidence. Damage from water and smoke will need to be repaired. The site will have to be inspected to ensure that the structure is sound.

3.2 HISTORY

By the eighth or ninth century, explosives were made in China from sulfur, potassium nitrate, and charcoal. Gunpowder first appeared in Europe in the 13th century.

One of the earliest recorded instances of a significant bomb attack was the attempt by Felice Orsini to assassinate Emperor Napoleon III with a sophisticated bomb in 1858. The Orsini attack used a sophisticated clockwork device manufactured in England. The device failed, and Orsini was captured.

In another example, Irish revolutionaries placed a large bomb against the wall of the Clerkwell prison in London in 1867. The bomb, containing 548 pounds of high-grade gunpowder, caused 12 fatalities and 120 injuries (Campbell, 2002, p. 79).

A significant change in the ability to use explosives for criminal purposes was the development of packaged explosives by Alfred Nobel in 1866. His creation, dynamite, was a boon to industry but also made criminal bombings easier and safer. Soon after the release of dynamite on the market, Irish revolutionaries became known as "Dynamitards" in recognition of their use of the new product (Campbell, 2002).

Anarchists and nihilists of the late 19th and early 20th centuries, along with ethno-nationalists like the Serbian Black Hand organization, used bombs to assassinate government officials and create terror in the public. They also used converted military explosive ordnance by fitting burning fuses to filled cannon balls, a technique that has been modernized in areas such as Iraq where artillery shells are modified for remote detonation.

Bombings continue to be the preferred weapon of terrorists and a common tool for criminals.

3.3 BOMB INCIDENTS

3.3.1 TYPES OF BOMB INCIDENTS

Accurate and consistent terminology is essential when defining and assessing vulnerability, security events, and mitigation treatments in relation to bomb incidents. The ill-informed use of a term may prejudice the process; for example, using the term *bomb hoax* suggests that the item or telephone call is already defined as fake before any evaluation has been conducted.

Bomb is often used as a generic term for a device designed to explode with force, causing damage and possibly injury. The more technical term is *improvised explosive device* (IED), defined as a (NATO, 2007, p. 130)

> device placed or fabricated in an improvised manner incorporating destructive, lethal, noxious, pyrotechnic or incendiary chemicals and designed to destroy, incapacitate, harass or distract. It may incorporate military stores, but is normally devised from non-military components.

The term also includes vehicle-borne IEDs (VBIEDs) and person-borne IEDs (PBIEDs).

The following definitions are used in this document:

- **Bomb:** an explosive or incendiary device designed to create damage and injury. A bomb can be made from commercial, military, or improvised (homemade) explosives and components. A bomb can be hand-delivered, vehicle-borne, part of a suicide attack, projected by a weapon, or delivered to the target by other means.

- **Unattended item:** an item whose presence is not readily explained and which could contain or be a hazard, such as a bomb.

- **Bomb threat:** a threat that a bomb has been or will be used against an organization or person.

- **Mail bomb:** an explosive or incendiary device sent through a postal or courier system.

- **Post-blast:** the scene after a bomb explodes, exhibiting damage and possibly death and injuries. An explosion is often called a bombing, but the term *post-blast* clearly refers to the scene after the bomb explodes.

- **Hoax:** an item or threat that does not actually represent a hazard but is designed to create the impression that a real bomb is on-site. The term *hoax* should not be used until the incident is finished and the summary report is written.

- **Secondary hazards:** materials on-site that are safe until affected by an explosion. Managers need to know the type and location of all hazardous materials and processes so emergency services can be briefed. Such information may be held in hazardous materials (hazmat) plans. Some items, such as high-pressure oxygen or water lines, may not be classified as hazmat but may still be secondary hazards. Some secondary hazards, such as fuel trailers, are mobile.

3.3.2 ELEMENTS OF A BOMBING

To develop a bomb incident management plan and apply bomb security management principles, it is necessary to understand the elements required for a bombing. They are motive, material, knowledge, and opportunity:

- **Motive.** The motive for using or threatening to use a bomb may be criminal (murder, extortion, intimidation, vandalism, etc); political (issue-motivated/cultural/terrorist, etc.); or personal (mental illness, disgruntled employee, domestic dispute, etc.).

  A review of possible motives may provide a basis for determining what sort of attacks may be expected and why they may be launched. For example, some perpetrators may desire the destruction of property but not the taking of life. Others may wish to create confusion and concern via threats, some intimidate for financial gain, and some want to kill.

- **Material.** A bomb requires a main charge of explosive or incendiary material; an initiator to detonate the explosive or ignite the incendiary; a triggering mechanism; and a safety switch. The components may be commercial, military, or homemade in origin.

- **Knowledge.** The knowledge required to build a bomb may be obtained through formal training provided to the mining and construction industries, pyrotechnic and special effects companies, and military and law enforcement agencies. Terrorist organizations, too, provide formal training in the manufacture and use of bombs. In addition, knowledge may be gained through personal research of texts and over the Internet. To successfully place a device on-site, the offender requires knowledge of the organization's activities, layout, and security measures. By contrast, little knowledge is required to make a bomb threat.

- **Opportunity.** The offender needs an opportunity to place the bomb on or near the targeted site or individual. This is the element that the organization can control through its bomb security management plan. It is possible to deny access to the site or deny the ability to bring explosive devices to the site (for example, through the use of detection systems).

3.3.3 ADVANTAGES AND DISADVANTAGES TO THE BOMBER

Bombs and bomb threats as a means of attack provide the perpetrator with advantages and disadvantages. Potential advantages to the offender include the following:

- large amount of damage compared to the size of the device

- greater level of damage than from an armed assault

- degree of anonymity, as the offender does not have to be on-site at the time of the explosion

- ability to cause damage with a device placed outside the site

- ability to cause considerable disruption to the organization's operation and reputation with little expense

- high media value for publicizing a cause

Disadvantages to the perpetrator, which may be advantages to the security manager, include these:

- possibility that the bomb maker will be killed by an explosion during construction or transportation of the bomb

- possibility that the bomb may not function as intended

- risk of detection when placing the bomb on or near the site or into a delivery system (mail or courier)

- risk that the device may be detected before it detonates, resulting in the evacuation of the site and possible disarming of the bomb

- forensic evidence from the bomb components, increasing the risk of identification and arrest

3.4 BOMB SECURITY PLANNING

3.4.1 BOMB INCIDENT MANAGEMENT PLAN

Each organization should develop a bomb incident management plan. The plan should provide information, policies, procedures, and training to limit the ability of a perpetrator to cause a bomb incident on the site. The plan should also help the organization respond appropriately to a bomb incident (including both threats and actual bombings).

The plan should provide specific guidance, policies, and procedures for fire wardens, security supervisors, and relevant managers. The plan must be site-specific but also be part of an integrated, whole-organization security management process. It should address unattended items, bomb threats, bombs, hazardous mail, and post-blast conditions.

For most organizations, the most likely types of bomb incidents are as follows:

In addition the plan should describe how training will be developed and delivered, in particular, training on the evaluation of bomb threats and unattended items and on search techniques.

The plan should be based on

- an understanding of the elements of a bombing: motive, material, knowledge, and opportunity;

- the exposure of the organization to bomb incidents due to its business environment, location, relationships, and staff;

- the effectiveness of emergency, health and safety, human resources, and other plans;

- current security measures; and

- senior management recognition of the risk of a bomb incident and the need for a plan.

3.4.2 **BOMB SECURITY AND SAFETY CONSIDERATIONS**

The principles of bomb security are as follows:

- **Preventing a bomb from entering the site.** This may be achieved through access controls and screening of visitors and goods, including mail. Where strict access control is not possible, access to critical areas on the site should be controlled.

- **Early detection of bomb incidents.** This depends on trained and aware staff with clear procedures for reporting items and threats.

- **Appropriate response measures.** These are based on clear and practiced procedures for evaluating bomb incidents and applying the relevant responses to protect people and the organization's assets and reputation. In some cases, the appropriate response may be to do nothing; in other cases, a full or partial evacuation may be required.

- **Careful design of facilities.** The right design can reduce the likelihood that a bomb could be brought on-site, increase the likelihood of detecting a bomb, and mitigate the effects of an explosion.

In particular, several measures can help an organization protect itself from a bomb incident:

- **Access control:** adequate boundary protection, personal identification and verification systems, electronic access control and recording systems, key control processes, restricting the public to public areas, etc.

- **Defense-in-depth:** additional levels of control and restricted access to higher-value assets

- **Good workplace practices:** keeping work areas tidy so that any items placed there are quickly detected

- **Staff awareness:** including the ability to detect and report items that are out of place

- **Training of supervisors and managers:** to respond appropriately to a report of a bomb

- **Standoff distance:** keeping assets far from the site boundary or, if that is impossible, compensating with other security measures, such as closed-circuit television or security patrols

- **Detection equipment:** appropriate to the task, deployed as part of a cohesive security plan, properly maintained, and used by trained staff

3.4.3 RELATED PLANS

Bomb security requires the cooperation of many business units, such as security, emergency management, facility management, human resources, occupational health and safety, environmental management, business operations, public relations, and finance. Those units may need to change their plans and operations to address bomb-specific considerations, such as evacuation distances and extended business disruptions. The security measures chosen must be appropriate to the organization's culture (relatively open, relatively closed, etc.).

3.4.4 GATHERING OF INFORMATION

To gauge its level of exposure to bomb incidents, an organization needs the following types of information:

- trends in bomb incidents
- details about the site (such as facility design and level of openness to the public)
- possible perpetrators
- specific people or sites that may be considered targets
- availability of explosive materials or ingredients
- possible changes to the working and political environment

Bomb incident information may be gained from a number of sources:

- open source media
- historical records
- organizational data
- professional organizations
- intelligence agencies
- national bomb data centers
- computer modeling
- corporate, national, and international liaison

3.4.5 BOMB RISK METHODOLOGY

To determine which prevention and response measures are appropriate, it is necessary to identify the likelihood of bomb incidents and the potential consequences should an incident occur. The likelihood of attack can be estimated by assessing the organization's changing profile and the security measures already in place. The consequences of a bomb incident may be assessed based on knowledge of the assets at risk and the potential effects of a bombing.

The risk assessment should be conducted early enough to enable procedures to be developed and practiced before they are needed operationally. The assessment will need to be revised as the environment changes and related security plans and site surveys are developed. Usually, each specific risk requires several preventive measures, and each measure may address several risks. To assess a threat, it may be appropriate to establish a threat evaluation team, which can assess all threats received by the organization, not just bomb threats.

3.5 BOMB INCIDENT MANAGEMENT

3.5.1 BOMB THREAT MANAGEMENT PRINCIPLES

Management must respond to bomb threats based on limited information and in limited time. The consequences of poor threat management range from an operational impact if an evacuation is called when not required to death if people are not evacuated in time.

The instinctive reaction to a threat may be to call an evacuation. However, evacuation is not always best. Constant evacuation undermines confidence in management's ability to provide a safe, secure, and productive work environment. It may also lead to copycat incidents as staff seek time off from work or outsiders enjoy the prospect of disrupting activities.

To respond effectively to a threat, the organization must recognize that it has been threatened, capture information about the threat and report it to the relevant authority within the organization, evaluate the threat, and respond appropriately.

Threat evaluation is a complex management decision that requires procedures, planning, training, and rehearsal. It is important that all employees know how to record the wording of any threatening call and how to forward a threatening e-mail or other message.

A threat can be evaluated for specificity (Newman, 2005, p. 6), which suggests the offender's level of knowledge and commitment. A detailed threat demonstrating knowledge of the site is more credible than a vague threat. Some callers warn the organization that they have placed a bomb—perhaps because the perpetrator wishes to damage property but not to kill, there has been a change of heart, or there is no bomb and the aim is instead disruption.

3.5.2 BOMB THREATS

A simple phone call threatening violence against an organization can cause massive disruption and fear. Moreover, the call costs the offender little effort and no special resources. The organization has little ability to prevent a threat from being made by telephone, e-mail, text message, mail, fax, or other communication method. Nevertheless, the organization can learn to recognize, evaluate, and respond to such threats. This section outlines considerations for developing a threat evaluation capability to determine the correct response to each threat.

Some organizations receive threats routinely, others at certain peak times, and others rarely, if ever. Those that are rarely threatened may be the mostly likely to stumble when it comes to bomb threat evaluation and response.

An effective threat evaluation process shows all stakeholders that the organization has a considered, practiced, and effective process for protecting the organization's assets either by evacuating when necessary or by minimizing disruption when the threat is not plausible. A threat is any claim that an act of violence will be perpetrated against the organization or an individual.

A process is required that permits the threat to be assessed by those with appropriate training and skills. The organization should regularly practice threat evaluation and carry out response exercises.

In a bomb threat assessment, the question is whether the threatener could have done what is claimed (e.g., placed a bomb on-site). A coordinated, trained, and practiced threat evaluation team (TET) can provide an effective capability to make the best decision on the information available at the time. Use of a team can bring different areas of knowledge to the evaluation, including a sound understanding of the site, its operations, and its security. A record keeper or secretary is an important member of the team, and a small team can act more quickly than a large team. The team's final decision should rest with the team leader.

Each site should have its own TET. It is difficult for someone off-site to have the required knowledge of the site's operations and security. Consideration should also be given to managing after-hours threats.

Threat evaluation consists of five *R*s:

- receive
- record
- report
- review
- respond

Receive

Threats may be received by phone, fax, mail, e-mail, or other means. In all cases, the organization should have a system for recognizing and capturing any threats. Staff, contractors, and possibly even visitors should know that management treats threats seriously and has a process for evaluating them. All staff should be educated in what to do if they receive a threat; this education can be through the organization's security awareness training, corporate newsletters, toolbox talks, intranet, or other mechanism.

Record

Evaluation relies heavily on the record of the threat made by the person who received it. Various threat checklists are available to aid in capturing useful information. Most are oriented toward bomb threats. National bomb data centers publish some of the best. For example:

- **U.S. Bureau of Alcohol, Tobacco, Firearms and Explosives**
  http://www.tn.gov/homelandsecurity/docs/bomb_checklist.pdf

- **Canadian Bomb Data Centre**
  http://www.rcmp-grc.gc.ca/tops-opst/cbdc-ccdb/telephone-procedure-eng.htm

- **Australian Bomb Data Centre**
  http://www.afp.gov.au/what-we-do/operational-support/australian-bomb-data-centre/bomb-safety-kit.aspx

The checklist should be widely distributed and easily accessed. Posting the checklist on the corporate intranet may ensure wide distribution, but the checklist may not be easy to find or use in a hurry. The checklist should be easy to use, provide adequate space for entering information, and be suitable for scanning or faxing (e.g., avoiding dark backgrounds and red printing).

All staff who deal with the public should be taught how to receive and record threats and to whom they should report the information. If the person making the threat begins a sentence and then changes it, the recorder should capture that change, which may be of value to the TET. The information should be recorded as soon as the call is completed.

E-mail, fax, and mail threats provide an accurate record of the wording of the threat but must still be captured and recorded (along with data on when and how they were received).

To avoid creating unnecessary concern, the person who received the threat should not to talk about it to others. The person must remain available to talk to the evaluation team and should be given a quiet place to sit while writing down any further details of the communication.

Receivers of threatening calls are often advised not to hang up—to facilitate tracing of the call. Each site should determine whether tracing is possible once the caller has hung up. If the phone has caller ID, then the number from which the threat is made should be recorded (Gips, 1999, p. 22). If the phone differentiates between internal and external calls, the origin of the call should be noted. If the call is received on a cell phone, the call log should be checked to see if the number of the caller was recorded.

Report

The threat should be passed to the TET quickly. Because the threat could be received by anyone, a simple and easily recognizable reporting line should be defined. One method is to ask staff to inform their local fire warden. Wardens may be advised to pass the information to the nominated manager and to begin preparing for an evacuation should one be called.

Policy should address whether the local supervisor should be advised of the threat. In most cases, supervisors should be informed but should not inform others. It may be of value for supervisors at different levels to participate in threat evaluation exercises so they understand the process.

The position to which all threats should be referred can be called the threat coordinator. A position, rather than a person, should be selected so that deputies and temporary appointments to the position may be trained in the responsibilities. This position chosen is often the security manager or the chief warden for the site.

The threat coordinator is responsible for calling together the TET. The threat coordinator conducts an initial evaluation of the threat and, if the threat does not permit time for a detailed evaluation by the TET, decides whether to initiate an evacuation. The threat coordinator should have sufficient authority to call other managers together at short notice and to evacuate the site.

In addition, the threat coordinator should understand the organization's emergency response procedures, be contactable at all hours (or share the duty with others so that a threat coordinator is on-site at all times), be on-site most of the time (not a frequent traveler), and have deputies who may fulfill the necessary functions.

The threat coordinator calls together the TET and coordinates the threat evaluation. Therefore, the threat coordinator should be able to do the following:

- Conduct the initial threat review and decide whether immediate evacuation is needed.
- If an immediate evacuation is not required, call together the TET.
- Gather the witness, the record of the threat, and all other relevant information.

Review

The review phase is the most important and difficult. Threat evaluation is a managerial decision-making process. Unlike a fire, a bomb threat is not a self-evident risk; it requires a review of facts to determine whether the threat is credible.

The primary evidence is the actual threat. Accuracy in capturing the wording of the threat is essential; the actual words used must be recorded, including omissions, changes in thought, slang, technical terms, or inaccuracies in terminology or knowledge of the site.

Other sources of information, too, can help evaluators assess whether the threatener could have done what is claimed. These sources include the following:

- closed-circuit television recordings
- access control records
- interviews with staff and others
- area searches ranging from employee scans of their work areas to formal searches of nominated areas
- knowledge of current events that may alter the organization's threat profile

The amount of time available for evaluating the threat can be calculated by subtracting the time required to evacuate the site plus a safety margin from the bomb deadline, if one is given. If the current time is 11:00 am and the deadline is noon, and it takes 20 minutes to evacuate the building, and a safety margin of 15 minutes is added, then the threat must be evaluated by 11:25 am, leaving only 25 minutes from the present time (D. Williams, 2005). If there is not enough time to evacuate the site and conduct a threat evaluation, then the threat coordinator should make an immediate decision on evacuation. If the perpetrator does not provide a deadline, the threat coordinator should evaluate the threat as quickly as possible.

The TET should consider why the perpetrator made the threat, which may also be considered a warning. It may be that the perpetrator wishes to damage property but not to kill; perhaps there has been a change of heart; or possibly there is no bomb and the aim is disruption, panic, and gratification for the threatener. A perpetrator wishing to kill is unlikely to provide a warning (unless ambush devices have also been placed). If a third party calls to state that he or she is not the perpetrator but is aware of the bomb, it may be that the perpetrator wishes to cause casualties, disruption, or damage, which the caller hopes to prevent.

It is important that the deliberations of the TET be recorded to assist with subsequent investigations, to justify the actions taken, and to provide a basis for future training and reviews of the process.

Respond

If it is deemed feasible for the perpetrator to have done what is claimed, then measures must be taken to protect personnel and the business, including evacuation of all or part of the site. Evacuation plans should include the closure of processes as well as the emergency transfer of data.

The TET should have a list of senior managers and others who should be promptly informed that a threat has been received and is being evaluated. The list could include the following if they are not part of the TET:

- manager of head or regional office
- site manager
- site's chief fire warden or emergency manager
- human resources manager
- senior union representative
- tenants
- manager of the threatened site if operated by a contractor

After-hours or alternate contact details should be available for each of the nominated positions.

Response options available to the TET include the following:

- If the threat is not plausible:
  — Continue working.
  — Advise the police that a threat has been received and assist with any investigations.
  — Advise staff and others who are aware of the threat that it has been carefully evaluated and the decision has been made to continue operations.
  — Complete the record of the evaluation and file it for future reference.

- If the threat is plausible:
  — Advise the police and if necessary request assistance with any evacuation.
  — Evacuate the site in coordination with the chief fire warden. Choose evacuation routes and assembly areas based on the threat.
  — Inform responding emergency services of the location of the emergency rendezvous point.

— Consider site security during the evacuation.

— Consider when and how the site will be reoccupied.

— Depending on the threat, consider implementing the business continuity plan. The evacuation may last for hours.

— Complete the record of the evaluation and file it for future reference.

In most jurisdictions, the making of a threat is a crime and should be reported to the authorities immediately. However, there is some risk that emergency services personnel may require an evacuation without access to all the information and without being aware of the financial and organizational implications of an unnecessary evacuation. Involving local emergency services in threat evaluation and response exercises may reduce this risk. The organization may wish to prepare media statements for release when threats are received.

3.6 BOMBS

The principles outlined here apply to all types of bombs: hand-delivered, vehicle-borne, mail bombs, suicide bombs, etc.

3.6.1 BOMB SECURITY PRINCIPLES

Several consequences could occur if a bomb entered a site:

- An explosion could occur. Its effects would vary depending on the construction, type, and location of the bomb.

- Operations could be disrupted if an evacuation is initiated.

- Personnel may face hazards (when descending stairs or crossing roads) during an evacuation.

- Staff, clients, and public may be concerned over how the incident was managed.

Even though a bombing may be assessed as unlikely for most organizations, the consequences of an explosion can be catastrophic, so appropriate mitigation treatments should be planned and implemented.

3.6.2 IDENTIFYING A BOMB

Identification of a bomb requires noticing that which is out of place and does not fit its environment. Because bombs are improvised, it is not possible to predict what they will look like or where they will be placed. Security measures may increase the chances of detection and thereby reduce the likelihood of a perpetrator trying to get a bomb onto the site. Particularly effective measures include access control to limit where the public can go, mail screening, and observant staff and members of the public.

All staff need to know how to report the discovery of a bomb—typically through the site's security or fire personnel. Those personnel must then know how to react to the report.

3.6.3 RESPONDING TO A BOMB

The planned response should include the following steps:

- Report the incident to the security manager or other selected position.

- Confirm whether the item has been clearly identified as a bomb as opposed to an unidentified item.

- If the item is believed to be a bomb, initiate an immediate evacuation.

- Supervise other aspects of the shutdown and evacuation in accordance with the organization's emergency procedures.

Protection from a bomb is achieved through distance and cover. If the bomb is located away from personnel, it may be best to keep them inside, based on hold-in-place or shelter-in-place procedures (Lee, 2007, p. 52). The decision must balance the exposure presented by evacuating people and the risks of leaving them in place. If people are kept in buildings, they must be moved away from any windows or glass facing the bomb and should use intervening walls as added protection. Only qualified bomb technicians should move the bomb or attempt to disarm it or make it safe.

More than one bomb may be on-site. Egress routes and assembly areas should be searched for unidentified items before or during the evacuation.

Personnel who saw the bomb or suspicious item should be available to brief the responding emergency services. A bomb can only be classified as a hoax by emergency services personnel or through subsequent forensic examination.

Where possible, the evacuation assembly areas should be at least 300 meters (328 yards) from the building, not in a direct line of sight of the bomb, not facing or under windows, and behind solid cover, such as another building.

3.6.4 **SUICIDE BOMBERS**

A person-borne IED or body bomb may be worn by the perpetrator in a suicide bombing or may be fitted to a victim, particularly as a negotiating point in a robbery, extortion, or kidnapping. Suicide bombs have been recorded since the late 19th century; their use escalated in the late 20th and early 21st centuries.

Organizations should conduct a formal threat assessment to determine whether they are likely to be the target of a suicide bomber (a very small subset of bombing offenders). Research into the motives and methods of suicide bombers may inform security managers concerned about this type of attack (C. Williams, 2004; Bloom, 2005; Pape, 2005).

Identifying and responding to suicide bombers is especially difficult, as they provide little time to respond and are guided weapons, capable of changing their target and timing. If a suspected body bomb is identified, usually the best way to minimize the consequences is to immediately begin to move people away and limit the bomber's ability to get closer to the organization's assets.

3.6.5 **VEHICLE BOMBS**

Vehicles enable a bomber to enter the targeted site with the bomb already prepared, thereby reducing the time the bomber has to spend on site. Vehicles also can be used to break through barriers, particularly if driven by a suicide bomber; vehicles tend to blend into the environment, making them difficult to identify as unusual; and vehicles can carry large quantities of explosives. Not all vehicle-borne IEDs (VBIEDs) are part of suicide attacks. The bombings of the New York World Trade Center (1993), the Edward P. Murrah Building in Oklahoma City (1995), and Khobar Towers in Saudi Arabia (1996) are examples where the drivers left the vehicles. Detection of a VBIED is difficult, particularly where public parking is provided.

Several security measures may limit the effect of vehicle bombs:

- forbidding public parking on-site, allowing only employees and other trusted personnel to park there

- removing or limiting parking near critical utilities or assets, or moving those items away from parking areas

- physically hardening critical utilities and assets close to public parking

- installing vehicle access barriers

- using fences, bollards, trees, terrain features, or other barriers to limit vehicle access to the site other than through controlled entry points

In cases where higher levels of security are required, the following may be considered:

- pre-registration of drivers and vehicles

- barriers at the inspection points, suitable for stopping forced entry, possibly with a second barrier behind the vehicle to prevent tailgating

- detailed inspection and detection procedures

- an isolation bay to the side of the inspection point but outside the barrier to enable the vehicle and driver to be segregated while additional inspections are conducted; it may need to be hardened or separated from the site's critical utilities or assets

- a turnaround area outside the barrier for vehicles that are not granted access

Many sites, particularly those in city centers, will not be able to apply these measures. In such cases, the site's perimeter should be hardened.

Related to VBIEDs are bombs placed in vehicles to kill the occupant. These are usually smaller devices positioned under the seat that the target is expected to occupy. Protective considerations against this type of attack include the following:

- secure garaging of the vehicle

- securing the vehicle when it is in public

- searching the vehicle before use and after it has been unattended

3.6.6 OFF-ROUTE BOMBS

Bombs can be used to attack vehicles in transit. Bombs have been buried under bridges (as in the assassination of Judge Giovanni Falcone in Sicily in 1992), placed on the side of the road, or fired from a distance with military or improvised rockets. Specially designed shaped charges and explosively formed projectiles, sometimes called off-route mines, have also been used to attack vehicles.

The primary protection measures include varying routes, keeping travel plans secure, training drivers and escorts to be aware of hazards, and identifying anything out of the ordinary. The *Protection of Assets* volume on security management contains a chapter on executive protection, which provides additional details on avoiding off-route bombs.

3.7 UNIDENTIFIED ITEMS

A common occurrence that can lead to significant disruption is the discovery of an unidentified item. This is an item that appears to have been left unattended. It may be a bomb, it may be an item forgotten or lost by the owner, or it may even be a piece of rubbish. Terminology is important; to refer to an item as suspicious before it is assessed prejudices the evaluation process. The item should be considered simply unidentified until it is assessed.

The likelihood of detecting unattended items increases if staff are trained, aware, and willing to identify and report such items. In countries that have suffered from sustained bombing campaigns, such as the United Kingdom, Spain, and Sri Lanka, members of the public are quick to report unattended items.

3.7.1 UNATTENDED ITEM PRINCIPLES

The question to be asked here is whether the item poses a hazard. A manager erring on the side of caution could decide to evacuate the site every time an item is found—greatly affecting the company. Instead, a process is required to help the manager determine whether the item is hazardous.

What is considered out of place varies from one area to another. An unattended school backpack in a public foyer, while worthy of investigation, may not be as worthy of concern as a backpack strapped to a gas cylinder. Still, the backpack in the public foyer must be evaluated, perhaps through video records (showing how it got there), as well as through interviews of staff and visitors.

If there is reason to believe an item is hazardous, it should not be touched. However, if the item's insides cannot be seen, no portable X-ray system is readily accessible, and the item seems likely to be lost property or rubbish, then it makes sense to open the item gently.

If the item is judged to be safe, it should be removed to the lost property area. If it is obviously hazardous or cannot be declared safe, then an evacuation away from the object should commence immediately. The authority to initiate an evacuation under these conditions should remain with the site's emergency control organization.

It is not the role of management or staff to decide that the item is a hoax; if it looks like a bomb or cannot be positively identified as safe, then it should be treated as hazardous. Only a bomb squad and forensic investigators have the skill and authority to determine if it is a real bomb. Once the evacuation is completed, the witness who saw the item should be available to brief emergency services.

Unidentified items can be recognized, reported, and evaluated quickly and discreetly if appropriate processes and training are in place. Some high-risk sites use portable X-ray systems.

3.7.2 ASSESSING UNATTENDED ITEMS

Unattended items can be evaluated using the same model as was proposed for bomb threats. The following principles apply:

- **Receive.** An unidentified item is received when it is found by a member of the public, a visitor, or a staff member. All those on site should be encouraged to report anything they believe is out of place.

- **Record.** The person finding the item should record as much information as possible as quickly as possible. The person should note where the object is, what it is, what it looks and smells like, whether it features any wires or aerials, and what activities were taking place in the area before the item was discovered.

- **Report.** The person finding the item should know how to report it to the appropriate person, possibly a fire warden, security officer, or supervisor. The person to whom the item was reported should know how to report the situation to the relevant manager.

- **Review.** The review of the item to decide if it poses a hazard must be done as quickly as possible. Determining how the item came to be there provides guidance as to whether it should be considered hazardous. It may be obvious from witnesses or CCTV footage that the item was accidentally left behind, that it was discarded as rubbish, or that it was deliberately placed there in a suspicious manner.

  Information on the item may be gained by interviewing staff or visitors; using the site intercom to ask anyone who may have left an item to return to that area; checking access control records; using portable X-ray machines; and reviewing CCTV footage of the immediate and surrounding areas. Awareness of bombing trends through liaison with law enforcement and security contacts may also help management determine whether an item should be considered suspicious.

- **Respond.** If the item is believed to be safe, it should be treated as lost property or rubbish. If it is deemed hazardous, the site should be evacuated in accordance with the bomb response plan.

3.8 POST-BLAST

If an explosion occurs, a post-blast response is required. The post-blast consequence management plan should take note of the following:

- The bombing is a deliberate act of violence, and the effects on staff and others may be considerable.

- If casualties occur, the organization's emergency medical and human resources support plans must be activated.

- The scene of the explosion will be a complex crime scene and may be isolated by the authorities for a considerable period.

- Structural assessments of the building may be required. The plan should state who will do these.

- The ability to obtain repair services, parts, and equipment maybe limited, particularly if the explosion affected a number of buildings in the area.

- Insurance may or may not cover the bomb damage.

- Legal protection may be required. A demonstrated adherence to planned bomb incident security management practices may assist with a legal defense.

If the explosion takes place outside the site, the organization may need to implement a hold-in-place plan so people can remain where they are until the nature of the hazard is identified and the most appropriate egress route and time for an evacuation can be determined.

3.9 HAZARDOUS MAIL

Hazardous mail includes not only bombs but also noxious and poisonous materials, acids, chemical or biological agents, and needles and blades (called sharps).

No workplace is immune to the risk of hazardous mail. Although the chance of receiving it is remote, businesses should put measures in place to detect and respond to hazardous items before they cause harm. In a survey of mail bomb policies, ASIS International found that only half the respondents offered mail bomb training and many lacked a comprehensive mail bomb security process (Harowitz, May 1997, p. 38).

The aim of the security manager should be to provide a safer and more secure work environment by increasing the ability to detect and respond to hazardous mail.

HAZARDOUS MAIL PRINCIPLES

The mail system offers a number of advantages to those wishing to cause injury and fear:

- Use of the mail provides some degree of anonymity.

- The item can be addressed to a specific individual or position within the target organization.

- Mail items come in a range of shapes and sizes, helping to disguise the contents.

- Millions of items of mail are processed each day.

The principle for mail screening is to identify that which does not fit its environment. The security manager may limit the perpetrator's opportunity to introduce an item into the workplace by identifying hazardous mail before it is opened. It is essential that all staff be trained in hazardous mail identification and appropriate response procedures. The families of senior executives and other higher-risk staff should also be instructed in mail screening, as they may receive hazardous items at home.

Limiting the number of locations where mail is opened minimizes the number of areas at risk. Where possible, the screening point should be placed in a location where discovery of a possibly hazardous item will result in minimal disruption to site operations.

Attacks by hazardous mail require the same four elements required in other types of bomb incidents: motive, material, knowledge, and opportunity. Motives are similar to those for other bomb incidents. Materials and knowledge to deliver bombs and other hazardous items through the mail are readily available. Opportunity is the element the security manager may influence. With appropriate mail screening and response processes, the likelihood that hazardous mail will reach the recipient and cause injury or concern can be greatly reduced.

EFFECTS OF HAZARDOUS MAIL

The most obvious effect of hazardous mail is death or injury. In addition, there may be disruption and ongoing fear and resultant workplace health issues, possibly affecting productivity. The company's reputation may be damaged due to a perception that the company failed to provide adequate protection. Another possible effect is litigation, particularly if management failed to apply appropriate protective measures.

Hazardous items sent through the mail are normally designed to function upon opening. It is unlikely that the item will have a time-operated fuse, as it is not possible to guarantee when the item will reach the intended recipient. The injuries caused by sharps, poisons, and noxious items are limited to a small population, while mail containing chemical or biological material may affect a larger number of staff.

3.9.3 **RECOGNITION OF HAZARDOUS MAIL**

The primary protection against hazardous mail is recognizing it before it is opened. The fundamental principles are identification, investigation, and response.

Identification

The following *EXPLOSIVE PARCEL* list details specific points of inspection when looking for hazardous mail (Australian Bomb Data Centre, 2009):

E xcessive securing material

e **X** cessive weight

P rotruding wires or tin foil

L opsided or unevenly weighted

O ily stains and discoloration

S tiff or rigid envelope

I s the package expected?

V isual distractions

E xcessive postage

P roper names and title incorrect

A ddress handwritten or poorly typed

R estrictive markings, e.g., "Confidential"

C ommon words missspelled

E ither unusual or foreign origin

L acks address of sender

The preceding identification points are based on indicators expected for an explosive or incendiary device and form a sensible basis for identifying other types of hazardous mail. Bombs have a number of basic components: a power source, often a battery, which can give the item an uneven balance; a firing switch, which may contain wires or foil; and an explosive or incendiary filling, which adds to the weight and may exude oil. The whole device is often mounted on a piece of card or wood and then heavily taped or tied to stop it from coming apart. The sender will try to ensure that the item is received and opened by the intended victim, hence the excessive postage, restrictive markings, and distractions to prevent proper examination.

People who send hazardous mail may not be in a balanced frame of mind, resulting in wrongly addressed, misspelled envelopes. Also, it is possible the sender has wrapped the bomb before addressing it, which may explain poor handwriting. Hazardous mail containing sharps may have a rigid feel, bumps, or uneven surfaces. Mail containing biological matter, acids, or other liquids will not feel like mail containing normal documents.

Investigation

If an item of mail is considered unusual, several methods may be used to determine if it should be considered hazardous. If the item has arrived though the mail system, it is unlikely to have a time switch, so there is time to gather additional information and calmly assess the situation. It may be useful to ask other staff or supervisors if they recognize the item, ask the recipient if the item is expected, and verify the return address.

A range of equipment can assist in mail screening. Each type has advantages and disadvantages for each particular workplace. In all cases, the equipment should only be used in conjunction with the skills of aware and trained staff.

Transparency sprays can be applied to envelopes to provide a degree of visibility of the contents. These sprays are inexpensive and may be effective on paper envelopes and wrapping. They do not work on all materials and can damage the documents inside. In some cases, using a spray to wet the packaging could weaken the wrapping and therefore increase the hazard.

Metal detectors are designed to indicate metal content within the item. The presence of metal does not mean a hazard exists, as normal mail often contains metal clips, binders, components, or packaging. Handheld metal detectors (wands) are not designed for mail screening.

Most explosive detectors work by taking a vapor or physical sample and subjecting it to a chemical analysis. These systems are designed as investigative tools where the presence of explosives is suspected and confirmation is required. Explosive vapor detectors are expensive and require staff to be properly trained. Some can also scan for drugs. Explosive detection sprays can indicate the presence of explosives with a reactive indicator. These systems are not intended for bulk screening and are best used as secondary screening tools.

X-ray machines come in a range of sizes and types. The volume of mail being processed determines the required capacity of the machine. Larger machines can scan whole mail bins at once. The X-ray machine does not need to be located in the mailroom; it may be better to screen incoming deliveries before they enter the mail center. X-ray machines raise some occupational safety and health implications, and businesses must ensure the machines meet all legal requirements and are maintained by qualified technicians. Effective use of X-ray machines requires staff to be trained in X-ray interpretation.

The detection of biological or chemical material in the mail is more difficult. An item may feel as if it contains grit, powder, liquid, or other unusual contents. Biological items can be sent through the mail without malicious intent but still pose a hazard. It is important that such items be detected prior to opening.

Response

The ability to respond safely to a mail bomb depends on proper procedures, which should address the following topics:

- reporting of the suspected mail bomb

- investigation as to why it is considered suspicious

- determining if it is considered hazardous or safe to open

- applying isolation measures if the item is deemed hazardous

- considerations for evacuating some or all of the site

In investigating the item, staff may need to compare the item to mail bomb recognition posters and similar guidance, ask the recipient if the item is expected, and check information on the sender, if any.

If the item has been delivered through the normal mail system, it has already been handled extensively, so one can probably move it safely, though it should not be opened. If it cannot be confirmed that the item has been delivered via the mail system, the item must not be moved and the area should be evacuated immediately.

Once an item is deemed hazardous, the following guidance applies:

- DO NOT open it, even a little, to see if it really is dangerous. The act of opening it or altering the packaging will probably cause it to explode, to release its contents, or to expose sharp objects.

- DO NOT wet the item (including immersing it in water) as this is likely to alter the packaging and may cause the device to function or the dangerous material to be released.

- DO NOT place the item in a container, particularly not in a locked one. This makes it difficult for the responding emergency services to access it and adds to the fragmentation risk as the box will be destroyed should the bomb explode.

- DO NOT invite other people to look at the item. Once the investigation reaches a stage where the item is considered hazardous, there is no need for additional people to be exposed to the potential risk.

- DO NOT carry the item through crowded areas. If it is to be moved, choose a route that will cause minimum disruption to the rest of the work force or public.

- DO place the item on a flat surface away from similar items so it can be readily accessed by the responding emergency services.

- DO consider moving the item to an isolation area. It may be possible to identify isolation areas that segregate the hazardous item from the workplace and public, enabling normal business functions to continue until emergency services arrive.

- DO gather as much information as possible about the item and its location for the responding emergency services, including why it is considered hazardous.

- DO evacuate the immediate area using the existing workplace emergency procedures (unless an isolation area is used).

- DO report it to the manager with the authority to control the incident.

- DO report it to emergency services, including police.

The primary protection from hazardous mail items is distance, which is achieved through evacuation. The evacuation plan for hazardous mail should address the following points:

- Partial evacuation may be appropriate, particularly if the item has been through the mail, as it is unlikely to function until opened. Emergency services will recommend if a full evacuation if required.

- In a bomb incident, the evacuation site must provide adequate distance and shelter.

- The plan should designate an emergency rendezvous point where the appropriate personnel can meet with and brief emergency services personnel.

- Neighboring businesses may need to be informed, particularly in a multi-tenant site. It can be disconcerting for neighbors to see others evacuating but not know why. Delay in evacuating other tenants may place them at unnecessary risk.

3.10 CHEMICAL AND BIOLOGICAL (CB) "WHITE POWDER" INCIDENTS

While not a new threat, white powder in the mail became a greater concern after the 2001 anthrax mailings in the United States. It is much more likely that a white powder mailing is a hoax than that it contains dangerous chemical or biological materials. Still, each such incident must be handled carefully.

3.10.1 EFFECTS OF CHEMICALLY OR BIOLOGICALLY CONTAMINATED MAIL

Hazardous biological or chemical material introduced to the worksite via mail may enter the building's airflow systems and contaminate the site. The onset of the illness or chemical effects may be instantaneous, or there may be a long incubation period. Anyone at the site may be at risk. Apart from the need to treat those obviously affected, a wider population will need to be examined and probably treated and decontaminated.

In the 2001 anthrax mailings, five letters containing a live biological agent were sent through the postal system in the United States. As a result, five people died from anthrax-related illness and many more reported for treatment, believing they were infected.

Organizations may receive unexpected biological or chemical materials for many reasons, such as in support of a claim or complaint or as a sign of disapproval. The receipt of such items will cause disruption. Those who have come in contact with the samples may be distressed and should undergo medical testing, and the site may have to be cleaned. Processes to detect and respond to hazardous mail should reduce the impact on staff and operations.

3.10.2 CB IDENTIFICATION

In most cases the hazardous material will not be detected until the item is opened and the material has been released. In some cases there may be indicators, in addition to the generic ones for hazardous mail, to suggest the presence of chemical, biological, or similar material, such as the feel of powder, fluid, or capsules in the item.

3.10.3 CB RESPONSE

When dealing with possible CB agents, the first goal is to limit the distribution of the material, and the second is to look after any staff who have been exposed. To prevent the spread of airborne material, the following steps may help:

- Separate the mailroom from the site's air conditioning or other circulation system.

- Then,

    — use a specially designed containment cabinet where mail can be opened and any contaminants trapped, or

    — place the item that is suspected of being contaminated in a sealable box or bag. or

    — cover the item where it is. It may be possible to place a large bag or bin over the material, thereby trapping the contaminant with minimum disturbance.

Regarding any personnel who may have been exposed, the following measures should be taken:

- Leave the contaminated area.

- Do not join the general population. Move to a nearby room, preferably one that has access to wash facilities and hands-free phones (so responding emergency services can speak to them and assess whether they need to be decontaminated).

- Wash hands and trap the water for later analysis.

- Accept counseling, if desired.

3.11 **COURIER-DELIVERED ITEMS**

Courier-delivered items raise additional concerns. They tend to arrive in the courier's envelopes or boxes, thereby disguising many potential identification features. They are delivered by hand and therefore could be fitted with a time fuse or anti-handling switches armed by the delivering courier. Consideration should be given to the following:

- Arrange for such items to be delivered to a single location where the staff may be familiar with the couriers and the types of deliveries expected.

- Inspect the item with an X-ray machine.

- Open the courier's envelope or box and inspect the contents for hazardous mail identification features.

- Have mailroom personnel deliver the item after inspection and confirmation with the recipient.

If there is any indication that a courier-delivered item is hazardous, it should not be handled and the area should be evacuated. The item should be treated as a bomb placed on-site, not as a mail bomb.

3.12 **SEARCH**

If there is a reasonable belief that a bomb is on-site, and there is adequate time before the deadline, some time should be spent trying to find the bomb. Otherwise the bomb squad is unlikely to come, and the site may have to be evacuated pending an explosion. If an evacuation was called and the deadline passes without incident, managers may consider asking the search teams to search all or part of the site before reoccupation. Search teams may also be used to check areas before important visits and meetings. Unless the site has a particular political value or is hosting VIPs, it is unlikely that the police will search the premises.

Searches may be conducted before, during, or after an evacuation, depending on the threat evaluation, type of business, time of day, current threat profile, and related considerations. Those who work in an area can best identify what is out of place there. They need a reporting chain and assurance that they are not being asked to put themselves at risk.

Searching is a skill that can be taught to staff. It offers a high degree of confidence that an item will be found or ruled out. Searchers are not necessarily looking for a bomb; they are looking for that which is out of place. They should know how to search a room quickly, identify what belongs there, and report their findings. When they find an item, they should know how to record the details and mark the route to the item for the benefit of the responding emergency services. Keeping areas tidy and restricting the public to public areas makes searches easier and more effective.

In search training, the use of replica bombs is not recommended for several reasons:

- In some jurisdictions, replica bombs are illegal.
- If someone not involved in the training finds the item, the incident may escalate, causing disruption to the organization.
- If the item is left behind after training, it may be found later, causing disruption.
- Bombs have many different appearances. It is counterproductive to train searchers to look for specific types of bombs.

Substitutes can be made from boxes or blocks of foam rubber, clearly marked as training aids. The location of the training aids should be recorded so they can be recovered later.

SEARCH MANAGEMENT

Searches must be carefully managed to ensure that all relevant areas are searched. There should be a central search coordinator, who may remain in the crisis control center but will determine which areas are to be searched and in what order and must decide when to withdraw search teams from the site to stay ahead of any deadline.

A search supervisor should be appointed for every three or four two-person search teams. The search supervisor should ensure that all rooms in the nominated area are searched in the time available, act as the communications link back to the search coordinator, and watch the time to ensure the search teams are withdrawn in accordance with the search coordinator's instructions. Supervisors should also know which staff have the knowledge to be able to search areas such as maintenance and equipment rooms, confined spaces, or high-security rooms.

Searchers should be pre-designated and provided suitable training. Emergency response packs should be available on each floor or search area. Each pack should contain, at least, a floor plan, flashlight, mirror, tape to indicate the location of any items found, pens, paper, chalk or adhesive labels to mark searched areas, gloves, search instructions, and the instructions for communicating with the search supervisor and search coordinator.

The search coordinator must be able to communicate with the search supervisors. The supervisors should be close enough to their search teams that they can communicate by voice. Radio and cell phone communication should be avoided as there is a possibility (however low) that radio transmissions could initiate an electric detonator. If radios are used, they should be used by supervisors in areas that have already been searched. Alternate means of communication include desk phones, emergency phones, and intercom systems.

If the bomb is well disguised and fits perfectly within the work environment, it is likely to remain hidden unless the search team is very well trained and has practiced extensively.

TYPES OF SEARCH

Several types of searches can be conducted:

- **Occupant search.** All staff members are taught how to look around their own work areas and report anything out of the ordinary. Nominated teams search external areas and engineering spaces. This type of search is suited to office and manufacturing sites with little public access.

- **Warden search.** Trained fire wardens, supervisors, or security personnel search an area and ask staff if they have observed anything out of the ordinary. This type of search is suited to public areas such as shopping malls and museums and may be done surreptitiously.

- **Team search.** Trained teams search nominated areas to gain information for the threat evaluation team. A team search provides a high degree of confidence but requires a higher level of training.

- **High-risk search.** This level of search requires considerable training and equipment and is undertaken by trained government personnel when there is a reasonable expectation that a bomb is on-site and it needs to be found before it explodes.

3.12.3 SEARCH TECHNIQUES

Search techniques should be taught face-to-face. The following are basic principles that may assist in developing a search capability:

- Search teams of two people work well as each team member can search an area while assisting the other and ensuring that between them all items in the allocated space have been searched.

- Search teams should leave at least one vacant room or area between them as they search. This will provide a degree of safety for teams should something untoward happen; more important, it provides a sound buffer between teams trying to search rooms.

- Utility and engineering spaces are best searched by those who work there and are familiar with the areas' fittings and fixtures.

- Upon entering a room or space, the search team should do the following:

  — Stop just inside the entrance and look and listen to become acclimated to the area. Doing so helps in identifying what fits in the area and what is out of place.

  — Divide the space into manageable sectors to enable a systematic and complete search. This may be done by height (ground to waist, waist to head, above head), by one member doing the walls and the other the center of the room, or by any other method that the space suggests.

  — Search all objects in the room (into, under, and above every item).

  — Use mirrors and other tools to look on top of or underneath objects.

  — Get down on hands and knees to look under objects to ensure nothing has been hidden or attached to the underside of furniture or fixtures.

  — Rather than standing on furniture, use steps or ladders if needed.

- After a room or area is searched, the team should mark the door to indicate it has been searched and report to the search supervisor that nothing was found. The search supervisor should mark that room off on the plan and allocate the next room.

- In some cases it may be possible to use CCTV to inspect areas such as passageways. CCTV records may also be used to check the passage of any unauthorized or suspicious visitors, thereby reducing the areas that need to be searched.

- Specific skills and considerations are required for searching cars, trucks, aircraft, watercraft, outdoor areas, and people.

Some search tools, such as mirrors, are inexpensive and can be distributed to all search teams. Others, such as explosive vapor detectors and nonlinear junction detectors (for detecting concealed electrical circuits), are expensive and require significant training and maintenance. Search dogs are of benefit if they are trained specifically in the detection of explosives and are managed by qualified handlers. All search tools should be evaluated against the organization's exposure and the ability of search teams to use the equipment correctly.

3.12.4 ACTIONS ON FIND

If an item is found during the search, decisions must be made on whether to continue the search, further investigate the item, or evacuate the searchers and others. This decision depends on where the item is found, why it is considered suspicious, and whether it matches the item described in the threat, if any. Searchers who discover an item should mark its location so the responding bomb squad can find it quickly. Options for marking include trails of paper, lengths of colored tape, and chalk marks.

If searchers find an item that seems out of place or is suspicious, they should do as follows:

- Do not touch it.

- Inform the search supervisor.

- Gain as much quick information about the item as possible: description, location, size, shape, sounds, smells, obvious markings, holes, antenna, etc. Digital photographs may help the responding emergency services.

- Mark the location of the item, using, for example, a roll of tape to mark the route from the item back toward the site entrance.

- Report to the search supervisor and remain available to be a witness to the responding emergency services.

When an item is reported by a search team, the search coordinator or equivalent will need to decide the following:

- whether to continue the search

- whether to continue searching in the same area as the reported item or to evacuate that part of the site

- which evacuation routes and assembly areas should be used, taking note of the location of secondary hazards and the pre-planned alternate routes

3.13 EXPLOSIVES AND EXPLOSIVE EFFECTS

3.13.1 EXPLOSIVES

Explosions may be mechanical, chemical, or nuclear. A mechanical explosion is the result of a buildup of heat and pressure inside a vessel. The pressure eventually overcomes the structural or material resistance of the vessel, and an explosion occurs. This mechanical explosion is accompanied by high temperatures, a rapid escape of gases, and a loud noise.

A chemical explosion relies on a chemical composition whose bonds can be broken easily, causing the material to become a gas very quickly. A gas occupies a greater volume than the original solid or liquid explosive and hence forces the surrounding air and material away from the center of the chemical change. Explosives differ in how fast they change from solid or liquid to gas. In a fire, solid material is converted to gas slowly, while in a chemical explosion the rate of change is measured in thousands of meters per second. The expanding gas tears apart the bomb's container and moves the parts and anything else nearby at high speed, creating high-velocity fragments. The explosion's heat may ignite any combustible materials nearby, especially if the bomb has been designed as an incendiary.

A nuclear explosion results from either the fission or fusion of atomic nuclei under extraordinary pressure. Nuclear explosions are orders of magnitude greater than conventional explosions. Weapons used during World War II used approximately 1 kg (2.2 lb.) of fissionable material to produce an explosion equivalent to 18.18 million kg (40 million lb.) of the chemical explosive TNT.

The United Nations classifies hazardous goods, explosives, and items containing explosives as Hazard Classification (HC) 1. Sub-classifications denote further details:

- HC 1.1: primary hazard is blast.

- HC 1.2: primary hazard is fragmentation.

- HC 1.3: primary hazard is fire.

- HC 1.4, 1.5, and 1.6: hazards are reduced by design or packaging.

In addition, explosive items are assigned to compatibility groups that indicate which items may be stored or transported with which others. The United Nations promulgates its classifications through its *Recommendations on the Transport of Dangerous Goods*, also called the Orange Book (United Nations, 2005), and the Globally Harmonized System of Classification and Labelling of Chemicals.

Explosives are roughly grouped into high and low explosives, depending on their velocity of detonation (VoD), which is the speed of the chemical change over a linear distance. Low explosives include propellants (e.g., gunpowders), pyrotechnic compositions, expelling charges for line throwers, and special effects systems. High explosives generate a detonation wave where the chemical change occurs without progressing through the burn stage; rather, the material is converted into a gas at a rate greater than 4,500 meters (14,700 ft.) per second. Low explosives are suitable for propelling and pushing; high explosives are used for shattering and for moving greater loads. The standard measure for explosive comparison is TNT (trinitrotoluene), which has a VoD of 6,900 meters (22,600 ft.) per second.

In most cases, an explosive's main charge is insensitive and requires the triggering of a more sensitive material for it to detonate or, in the case of a low explosive, to ignite. Therefore, most explosive devices consist of a detonator or igniter that is reasonably easy to initiate via shock, friction, or heat; an intermediary charge to increase the effect of the detonator or igniter; and a main charge, which may be high or low explosive, an incendiary, or a mixture of these.

3.13.2 EXPLOSIVE EFFECTS

To plan for bomb incidents, one must understand of the effects of an explosion. Explosive effects may injure and kill people, damage IT equipment, cause structural damage, remove sprinkler heads and damage water pipes, disrupt building services, and hinder rescue and emergency responses.

The three primary products of an explosion are blast, fragmentation, and heat.

Blast

The gas released from the chemical breakdown requires considerably more volume than the initial explosive, so it moves away from the site of the explosion. The rapid expansion of gas (the blast wave) breaks and destroys surrounding structures and people. The wave can be thought of as a wall of compressed air traveling close to the speed of sound. Immediately behind the blast wave is a low-pressure area from which the compressed air was drawn. This low-pressure area (sometimes incorrectly called a vacuum) further damages structures weakened by the blast wave by causing them to stress in the opposite direction.

Blast is applied to an object either (1) through the sudden increase in pressure (peak incident pressure) that passes through the object, or (2) by applying pressure increasingly until the object fails or the blast is reflected (peak reflected pressure).

The nature of the blast wave depends on several variables:[1]

- **Type of explosive and method of detonation.** A military-grade high explosive has different work properties than an agricultural explosive, such as an ammonium nitrate and fuel oil (ANFO) mixture. The rapidity with which an explosive develops its maximum pressure is a measure of its brisance. A brisant explosive is one in which the maximum pressure is attained so rapidly that the effect is to shatter any material in contact with it and all surrounding material.

- **Location.** Reflecting surfaces near the site of the explosion can increase the effect of the blast wave. Also, the proximity of combustible materials and other secondary hazards can augment the effects of the explosion.

- **Packing or confinement.** If the explosive is packed in such a way that a great pressure is required to cause a release from the container, the initial blast effect will be greater than that from unconfined explosion. The strength, material, and shape of the confining container affect the size, velocity, and trajectory of the explosion.

For example, 1 kg (2.2 lb.) of TNT, placed on the ground without any confinement and correctly detonated, will apply approximately 43 kilopascals (6.2 psi) to a wall 5 m (16.5 ft.) away about 8 milliseconds after detonation. If the wall does not fail, the pressure builds up to more than 100 kilopascals (14.5 psi) (U.S. Army Corps of Engineers, 1992).

In an explosion, the pressure rises from the ambient pressure in the room to peak pressure within milliseconds as the shock front and blast wave pass over the observer. After the blast wave passes, the low-pressure phase occurs. The accompanying picture shows the effect of the shock front and blast wave and then the negative pressure phase.

---

[1] This is a simple summary of a complex topic. Technical information on blast effects is available from such organizations as the International Association of Bomb Technicians and Investigators, the Institute of Explosive Engineers, and the International Society of Explosives Engineers.

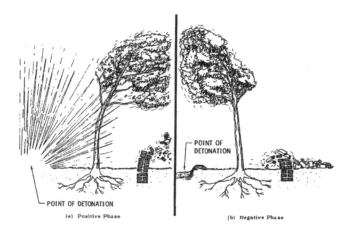

(a) Positive Phase   (b) Negative Phase

The blast wave dissipates quickly (based on a cube-root scale), so the greater the distance between the bomb and the target, the greater the protection from bomb effects. The same 1 kg TNT explosion mentioned earlier will apply only 8.6 kilopascals (1.2 psi) to a wall 15 meters (50 feet) away. Distance provides a significant benefit in bomb prevention and response.

Fragmentation

The casing of the bomb and anything nearby will be shattered and turned into projected fragments. In some cases, the bomb is designed to enhance the fragmentation effect through the addition of nails or similar items.

Fragmentation from the bomb casing, including parts of the vehicle if it is a vehicle bomb, and from failed structures nearby can be projected considerable distances. The lethality of the fragments depends on their mass and velocity and the resilience of the target structure (including vehicles and people).

Fragments travel away from the seat of the explosion in a straight line before being acted on by gravity and air resistance. Therefore, the likelihood of being struck by a fragment is related to distance.

Heat

The detonation process is exothermic and generates considerable heat. For many explosives, this heat does not last for long and is unlikely to start a fire unless combustibles are nearby or the bomb has been designed with added accelerants. Some bombs are specifically designed as incendiaries.

3.13.3 **BLAST/INJURY TABLES**

Figure 3-1 shows the distances at which injuries from a blast can be expected for a bomb of a given size. Any person within the stated range can be expected to suffer the indicated injury. The calculations are based on an unconfined, hemispherical explosion at sea level with no vertical reflecting surfaces.

The actual effects depend on such variables as location, reflecting surfaces, and bomb construction. Injury to people is also related to the blast impulse, that is, the time during which the pressure is applied to the body. In bombings the impulse time is usually 6-9 milliseconds.

Figure 3-1 does not take into account fragmentation effects (addressed in Figure 3-2) or injuries sustained when a body is physically projected by the blast wave. Figures are drawn from a number of U.S. and Canadian studies (for example, L'Abbe, 1989, and U.S. Army Corps of Engineers, 1992).

Explosive weight of bomb	Threshold eardrum rupture	Threshold lung damage	Slight risk of death	High risk of death
2 kg (4.4 lb.)	8m (26 ft.)	3m (10 ft.)	1.7m (5.5 ft.)	1.2m (4 ft.)
5 kg (11 lb.)	10.6m (35 ft.)	4m (13 ft.)	2.3m (7.5 ft.)	1.75m (6 ft.)
10 kg (22 lb.)	13.4m (44 ft.)	5m (16.5 ft.)	3m (10 ft.)	2.2m (7 ft.)
25 kg (55 lb.)	18m (59 ft.)	6.8m (22 ft.)	4m (13 ft.)	3m (10 ft.)
Conversions are approximate.				

Figure 3-1
Blast Effects

The assumptions are:

- threshold pressure for eardrum rupture = 30 kilopascals (4.35 psi)

- threshold pressure for lung damage = 200 kilopascals (29 psi)

- slight probability of death = 700 kilopascals (101 psi)

- high probability of death = 1300 kilopascals (188 psi)

- explosive weight is in TNT as an international standard

- unconfined, hemispherical blast with no vertical reflecting surfaces

In Figure 3-2, the fragmentation modeling was conducted using computational fluid dynamics and related software (Morrison & Williams, 2004). The calculations are based on a car bomb with explosive charge weights of ammonium nitrate and fuel oil (ANFO).

	Bomb Size (kg)				
	10 (22 lb.)	20 (44 lb.)	50 (110 lb.)	100 (220 lb.)	200 (440 lb.)
Range (m)	**Probability of Death (%)**				
5 (16.5 ft)	100	100	100	100	100
10 (33 ft)	28	34	49	97	100
20 (66 ft)	6.9	8.5	12	24	49
50 (165 ft)	1.1	1.4	2	3.9	7.8
100 (330 ft)	0.04	0.07	0.13	0.25	0.5
500 (1650 ft)	0.001	0.003	0.008	0.02	0.03
Conversions are approximate.					

Figure 3-2
Fragmentation Effects

3.14 EMERGENCY MANAGEMENT CONSIDERATIONS FOR BOMB INCIDENTS

Emergency response planning should address the following:

- **Shelter.** A hold-in-place or shelter-in-place procedure (to keep people inside if the threat is external) is needed, including access to water, washrooms, food, and communications (Lee, 2007).

- **Data search.** It may be useful to bring access control and visitor records to the assembly area so a check of all those recorded as being on-site can be conducted. This can possibly be done through remote IT access.

- **Assembly areas.** These are places where personnel can stay out of the weather, preferably with access to amenities.

- **Special item removal.** It may be necessary to evacuate information, equipment, laboratory samples, or other items from the site.

- **Alerting of neighbors.** If an evacuation is initiated, neighbors should be notified by either the organization or the responding emergency services. An effective threat evaluation capability will help protect against any claims from others that they were needlessly inconvenienced by the decision to evacuate or were put at risk because of a decision not to evacuate.

- **Shutdown procedures.** Failure to shut down certain processes during an evacuation can be costly and hazardous. In some industries, such as petrochemical processing, evacuating the site's main control room may generate a greater hazard than that posed by the bomb. On sites where food is prepared, it may be necessary to close down cooking fires and gas lines to reduce hazards. On sites such as refineries, specially designed bunkers may be used to allow ongoing control during critical incidents.

- **Security.** In larger sites, areas not related to the location of the device could be locked to provide security during the evacuation.

- **Emergency rendezvous point.** The location of an emergency rendezvous (ERV) should be selected in advance. At the ERV, the witness, a senior manager, the threat evaluation team leader, the chief warden, and preferably the site engineer can meet and brief responding services. Accurate site plans, including the location of secondary hazards, should be brought to the ERV. Prompt, accurate information may help the emergency services save the company's facility.

Unlike a fire, a bomb incident may result in reoccupation of the site, particularly if there is no explosion. The following reoccupation considerations should also be included in the emergency plan:

- **Decision.** The responding emergency services may provide advice on reoccupation, but the final decision is likely to rest with the organization's management.

- **Search.** It may be advisable to search a site or selected areas before reoccupation, especially if a credible threat was received but no bomb was found before the evacuation.

- **Clients and customers.** Clients and customers may be required to stay in the assembly areas. Depending on the time of day, it may make sense to let staff disperse and return later or the next day, in which case a communication system, message center number, Web site, or other method may be required. Safe transit to their vehicles must be ensured. In remote areas, it may be necessary to arrange for buses to move people to public transportation.

3.15 **BLAST-PROTECTIVE DESIGN CONSIDERATIONS**

Physical design considerations may assist in deterring, detecting, and responding to bombs as well as reducing the effects of an explosion. These considerations should be kept in mind when a new site is being designed or refurbishments are proposed.

The principles of crime prevention through environmental design (CPTED, addressed in the *Protection of Assets* volume on physical security, apply also to bomb security. Good sight lines, adequate lighting, clear access routes, and other design elements make it easier to identify suspicious activity and unattended items.

Research into engineering design of blast-resistant structures is ongoing (Mendis, 2005). Where possible, distance should be provided between the site's assets and public areas. At a minimum, critical assets and functions should be separated from public areas and protected by at least two walls (that is, they should not border public areas).

The use of films and other technologies to reduce glass fragments should be assessed against the possible and probable location of bombs, the expected size of a bomb on the site, and the assets, including people, near the glass. Anti-shatter technologies should take into account the type of glass, its expected failure mode, how the glass is fitted to the frames, and how the frames are fitted to the building. If the explosion is outside the building, glass close to the explosion can be expected to enter the building, while glass further away may be stressed by the blast wave and then drawn away from the building by the negative pressure.

Trash bins have been used to conceal bombs, but removing bins may lead to an increase in other hazards, such as trips and falls, contamination, and infestations. Their use in public areas may need to be limited if key assets are nearby. If situated correctly, special bins can direct a blast away from people.

A requirement that visitors store their bags in a cloakroom may reduce the risk that a bomb could be brought on-site, particularly if it is a stated policy that staff may look into any bag as a condition of storage. A perpetrator is unlikely to bomb a cloakroom even if it is in the targeted building. Still, cloakrooms should not be established near utility lines or other critical assets. Also, staff should be taught how to request the opening of bags, in accordance with local law, and how to identify and respond to possibly hazardous items.

As an example of the use of distance, observation, and response measures, the 1996 bombing of the U.S. military accommodation building at Khobar Towers in Saudi Arabia was limited in its effect because of the security management measures in place. The bomb is estimated to have contained approximately 907 kilograms (10 tons) of explosives. The size of the bomb was a response to access control measures that denied the offenders the opportunity to get close to the building. A guard watching the perimeter noticed a tanker truck and determined that it was out of place and potentially a hazard. An evacuation was immediately initiated. Only 19 service personnel died. Without the bomb detection and response, casualties would have been considerably higher.

3.16 SUMMARY

Bomb incident management is more successful when careful planning has taken place. Security professionals and others given the responsibility for protection strategies should make every effort to consider this topic during their normal emergency preparedness discussions. Those who fail to consider this type of act and incorporate countermeasures into the design of a comprehensive security program may experience greater chaos should an incident occur.

REFERENCES

Australian Bomb Data Centre. (2009). *Bombs: Defusing the threat.* Canberra: Australian Federal Police. Available: http://www.afp.gov.au/~/media/afp/pdf/b/bombs-defusing-the-threat-bookmarked-version.ashx [2011, August 12].

Bloom, M. (2005). *Dying to kill: The allure of suicide terror.* New York, NY: Columbia University Press.

Campbell, C. (2002). *Fenian fire: The British government plot to assassinate Queen Victoria.* Hammersmith, United Kingdom: HarperCollins.

Gips, M. (1999, June). Defusing threats. *Security Management.*

Harowitz, S. (1997, May). Dangerous deliveries. *Security Management.*

L'Abbe, R., et al. (1989). Blast effects, Parts 1-4, *The Detonator,* Vol. 16, No. 6, and Vol. 17, Nos. 2, 4, and 6. Colorado Springs, CO: International Association of Bomb Technicians and Investigators.

Lee, J. (2007, January). Gimme shelter, *Security Management* [Online]. Available: http://securitymanagement.com/article/gimme-shelter [2008, August 29].

Lee, J. (2007, January). Gimme shelter. *Security Management.*

Mendis, P., Crawford, J., & Lan, S. (2005). *An introduction to explosion effects and design for blast.* Sydney, Australia: Advanced Protective Technologies for Engineering Structures.

Morrison, R., & Williams, D. (2004.) Effects of large vehicle bombs. Presentation to International Association of Bomb Technicians and Investigators, Australian Chapter Training Conference, Canberra, Australia.

Newman, G. (2005). *Bomb threats in schools.* Washington, DC: U.S. Department of Justice, Office of Community Oriented Policing Services.

Pape, R. (2005). *Dying to win: The strategic logic of suicide terrorism.* New York, NY: Random House.

United Nations Economic and Social Council, Committee of Experts on the Transport of Dangerous Goods. (2005). *Transport of dangerous goods: Recommendations of experts on the transport of dangerous goods* (UN Orange Book), 14th ed. New York: United Nations.

U.S. Army Corps of Engineers. (1992). *Design and analysis of hardened structures to conventional weapons effects.* TM 5-855-1. Vicksburg, MS.

Williams C. (2004). *Terrorism explained.* London: New Holland Publishers.

Williams, D. (2005, March/April). Dealing with explosive situations: Learning how to manage a bomb threat. *Security Oz.*

INDEX

A

al Qaeda, 44, 46
all-hazards, 7, 10, 19, 44
alternates in emergency planning, 8, 13, 16, 17, 20, 22, 24, 34, 68
anthrax, 40, 47, 81
Aum Shinrikyo, 47
Australia, emergency management in, 4, 65, 77

B

biological terrorism. *See* CBRN terrorism
blast effects. *See* explosives and their effects
blast-protective design, 94
bomb identification, 69, 71, 73, 74, 76, 77, 94
bomb incident management plan, 10, 30, 58, 60
bomb response, 7, 11, 55, 61, 64, 68, 70, 74, 79, 90, 94
bomb search, 60, 67, 70, 83, 84, 93
bomb security, principles of, 61, 63, 69, 73, 76, 77, 85, 94
bomb threats, 10, 55, 56, 58, 59, 60, 63, 85, 93
bombs. *See* explosives and their effects
bombs, terminology, 57, 73
business continuity, 2, 4, 6, 7, 9, 11, 33, 55, 69
business impact analysis, 7, 11, 33

C

Canada, emergency management in, 3, 65
Caribbean, 4
CBRN (chemical, biological, radiological, and nuclear) terrorism, 46, 47, 75, 76, 78, 79, 81, 87
command and control, 16, 17, 21
communications, emergency, 6, 12, 21, 28, 34, 84, 92
continuity of operations (COOP), 9, 11, 33
counterproliferation, 47

counterterrorism, 44, 45
crime prevention through environmental design (CPTED), 94
crisis management center. *See* emergency operations center
crisis management team. *See* emergency management team
cyberterrorism, 48, 49, 50

D

Department of Homeland Security (DHS), 2, 19, 21
disabilities and emergency planning, 14, 29
drills and practice, emergency management, 12, 30, 61, 84
dynamite, 56

E

emergency management structure, 3, 16, 17, 18
emergency management team, 12. *See* crisis management team
emergency management, key elements of, 6, 14, 17
emergency management, terminology, 2, 6
emergency operations center (EOC), 20
emergency operations plan (EOP), 2, 5, 7, 10, 14, 18, 33
emergency response agencies, 4, 12, 13, 23, 26, 75
emergency, types requiring planning, 1, 8, 9, 60
evacuation, 3, 4, 10, 12, 15, 28, 29, 30, 55, 59, 63, 66, 69, 73, 75, 79, 80, 82, 87, 92
exercises. *See* drills and practice, emergency management
explosives and their effects, 10, 16, 23, 30, 40, 47, 48, 50, 55, 56, 57, 75, 78, 87, 88, 90, 91, 94

F

Federal Emergency Management Agency (FEMA), 2, 3, 6, 10, 19, 25

G

H

hackers. *See* cyberterrorism
hazmat (hazardous materials), 8, 9, 10, 28, 30, 58, 75, 81
history of emergency management, 1

I

improvised explosive device (IED), 10, 57, 71
Incident Command System (ICS), 17

J

jihad, 43, 44

K

L

logistics and resources, emergency, 17, 26, 31, 34

M

mail, hazardous, 58, 60, 75, 81
mitigation, 2, 6, 11, 33, 69
mutual aid, 24, 31

N

National Fire Protection Association (NFPA), 3
National Incident Management System (NIMS), 19
National Institute of Standards and Technology (NIST), 3
New Zealand, emergency management in, 4
Nobel, Alfred, 56
nuclear terrorism. *See* CBRN terrorism

O

Occupational Safety and Health Administration (OSHA), 19, 62, 78

P

planning. *See* emergency operations plan (EOP)
post-blast, 58, 60, 75
preparedness, 3, 7
public affairs/media relations, 14, 17, 19, 24, 62

R

radiological terrorism. *See* CBRN terrorism
records, vital business, 34, 48
recovery, 5, 7, 9, 31
resilience, 4, 33
response, 7, 10, 19
risk assessment, 8, 11, 62, 63

S

search. *See* bomb search
shelter-in-place, 12, 14, 30, 70, 92
shutdown, emergency, 14, 31, 93
suicide bombers, 57, 69, 71

T

terrorism, analytical approaches to, 42
terrorism, definitions, 41, 47
threat evaluation team, bomb, 63, 64, 65, 67, 93

U

unidentified/unattended items, 57, 60, 70, 73, 74, 94
United Kingdom, emergency management in, 3, 73

V

vehicle bombs, 71, 90

W

weapons of mass destruction (WMD), 40, 45, 47
white power incidents. *See* anthrax

XYZ

X-ray, 73, 74, 78, 82